MAKING
MOLEHILLS
out of
MOUNTAINS

Leadership Strategies
for Conquering
Life's Summits

ANDREW McCREA

BLAKE
& KING

Maysville, Missouri

Published by Blake & King
5650 Berlin Road
Maysville, MO 64469

Publisher's Cataloging-in-Publication Data
McCrea, Andrew

Making molehills out of mountains: leadership strategies for conquering life's summits/ Andrew McCrea. – Maysville, MO : Blake & King, 2008.

p. ; cm.
ISBN: 978-0-9725331-5-7

1. Leadership 2. Success in business. 3. Achievement motivation I. Title.

HM1261.M33 2008
303.3/4—dc22   2007935969

Project coordination by Jenkins Group, Inc.
www.bookpublishing.com

Interior design by Debbie Sidman
Cover design by Chris Rhoads

Printed in the United States of America
12 11 10 09 08 • 5 4 3 2 1

Dedication

*To my sister, Jill, who shows us how little steps
can scale the biggest mountains in life.*

Contents

CHAPTER I

The Journey Begins

SPRINGDALE, TENNESSEE

"The journey of a thousand miles begins with one step."

—LAO-TSE

I t was a warm spring day in the Smoky Mountains of Tennessee. The sunlight gently reflected off the green of new buds bursting from the timber-lined ridges. The redbuds were also coming to life, and the mix of reds, greens, and yellows signaled that the woods and surrounding fields were awakening from their winter rest.

My trip down Route 25 East had begun the day before when I landed at Blue Grass Field in Lexington, Kentucky. I was told that the car I rented was not available and that in exchange for the inconvenience, I would be upgraded to a better model. When I arrived at the rental car lot, I was excited to find that my upgrade was to a new black Ford Mustang convertible.

Now, with the top down, I was making great time on my way to another broadcast assignment. I knew that Route 25 East would take me all the way to my destination, but now I was beginning to doubt my own directions. Not only should I have arrived 10 minutes ago, but also I had just gone through two towns on Route 25 that were not on the map. Granted, they were small towns, but something seemed amiss, and that was confirmed when I rolled into a town of 3,000 people that should definitely have been pinpointed on my map yet wasn't.

After some careful searching, I found that the city was in fact on my map and it was on Route 25—Route 25 West. When you need to drive two hours east, reaching your destination on a road called 25 West is rather difficult. For the past half an hour, I had enjoyed the view and relished the speed of my Mustang that was taking me farther and farther from my destination. The only thing left to do: turn around.

Turning around was the only thing I could do if I wanted to get to my destination. It didn't matter how pretty the day was or how fast I could accelerate in my convertible; all I would accomplish would be heading farther in the wrong direction if I did not stop and get my bearings.

Yet in real life, we sometimes don't give as much thought to our destination. We might fail to turn around. This book is about destinations. It is about the goals and plans we have for our lives. It is a book about how we can reach those destinations and how we can help others reach their destinations as well.

But this book is also about the drive. It is about how we get to those destinations in the most efficient and effective way possible. The destination and the drive must go together. If you have a destination without the drive, you will have goals to achieve, but you will never see those dreams fulfilled. If life were about just the drive, you would develop skills that would make you an effective and efficient leader, but you would never be headed toward achieving any specific goal. Think about it: if life were about just the drive, you would have been given the tools to move as fast as possible in the exact opposite direction you needed to go!

Moving toward our destination requires us to make turns in our lives. At times we may need to stop and make a complete U-turn. Making changes now creates lifelong habits that move us in the right direction. It's important for each of us to consider the turns we need to make in order to make our drive to the destination the most direct route possible.

Putting our destination and our drive together can create great results. It turns something ordinary into something extraordinary. It helps us make positive changes in our own lives and the lives of those around us. Together, destination and drive help us achieve our goals.

What do destination and drive together look like? I was recently staying at a hotel on the Atlantic Coast, and before going to bed, I called down to the front desk to see whether anyone happened to know what time the sunrise would be the following morning. The clerk checked the local paper and told me that the sun would rise at 4:54 a.m. I thanked the clerk for looking up the time and then set my alarm clock for 4 a.m.

After just a few hours of sleep, I quickly pulled on my clothes, went to my car, and drove for about 30 minutes. I arrived at a small parking lot at 4:45 that morning. A pink glow was already on the horizon, indicating that the appearance of the sun was just a few minutes away.

Not too many people get up at 4 a.m. just to see the sunrise. If you do get up that early *just* to see the sunrise, either you are a little crazy or that particular sunrise must have something pretty special about it. In my case, both might be true.

At 4:54 that morning, I was standing at the pinnacle of Cadillac Mountain in Acadia National Park on the coast of Maine. It is said that if you are standing on top of that mountain at sunrise, you are high enough in elevation and far enough east on the continent that you will be the very first person in all of North America to see the sun that day.

On most clear days from spring through fall, several dozen people will make that trip to the mountain to see the sunrise. The sunrise is beautiful as it appears over the islands dotting the rocky shoreline,

Sunrise from the summit of Cadillac Mountain, Maine

but it is the same sun that any of us could wake up and see almost any morning where we live. But there is something special about this particular sunrise. It is something so special that people will drive for hundreds of miles just to see it.

When you have the perfect destination and you combine it with the right drive, you can be the first person on the continent to see the sun. When we combine destinations and drive in our own lives, we learn how average individuals can make lasting differences in their homes, schools, and communities. It is the ability to take something we may take for granted, such as a sunrise, and make it something special, like a sunrise on Cadillac Mountain.

If our destinations are mountains that must be climbed, we can take a series of steps to improve our odds of reaching the summit. Although most of us take for granted the process of getting in our car and driving somewhere, several unconscious decisions go into that everyday scenario. At some point in our lives, we had to learn how to drive. We had to pass a driver's test. We had to earn money to buy a car. We have to earn money to buy gas and insurance for the car. We have to figure out when to get on the road to avoid traffic. We think about what errands we need to run and when we will make those trips.

What is a simple everyday process does involve several steps. Leadership is much the same. Deciding to pursue our dreams takes motivation. Developing the goals we want to achieve takes time and forethought. We have to learn to make the most of our time. Working with others to meet these goals becomes important. We learn personal and team leadership skills to better accomplish our tasks. We live our lives to leave a lasting impact on our families and our communities. Leadership is composed of many steps that we may take for granted.

Effective leadership helps turn the mountains in our lives into molehills. This doesn't mean that we settle for smaller goals; it simply means that we learn and apply the skills that make climbing those big mountains in our lives easier. It also means we gain a new perspective on how we work with others.

In Bedford County, Pennsylvania, there is a famous destination called Gravity Hill. Each year hundreds of people drive there because their car seemingly rolls uphill! It's a fascinating illusion. Cars don't actually defy gravity, yet because of the slope of the surrounding countryside, the eye perceives that the car is rolling uphill when, in fact, surveyors' measurements will show that the road actually has a slight decline.

In the leadership world, we are sometimes our own worst enemies. We may believe that giant obstacles exist when, in reality, they aren't the big challenges we once imagined. That's why the cliché "making a mountain out of a molehill" exists. We get caught up in looking at the scenery around us and convince ourselves that the summit cannot be reached. Perhaps it's a combination of learning new leadership skills and gaining a new perspective on the summit ahead.

That's why this book's title is "Making Molehills out of Mountains." The strategies in this book provide ways we can break down some of the challenges and illusions that surround effective leadership and show us how we can apply proven leadership steps to achieve more in life. Our goal is to turn the cliché upside down and develop habits that bring success.

This book talks about those steps and how we can use them to better work with and lead others. There will be plenty of real-life examples of how people put leadership into practice and how we can learn to do this as well. Together, these points and personal examples provide a road map for the destination we seek to visit and the drive we seek to make.

> You will find that the point, or moral, of each chapter in this book is included in a shaded box with a compass symbol. The first compasses were used by the Chinese almost 2,000 years ago. They used lodestone, a mineral composed of iron oxide that aligns itself in a north-south direction. These natural magnets were eventually placed on squares with directional markings. Once navigators found north, they immediately knew how to find east, south, and west.

The shaded boxes in this book work much the same as does a compass. These simple points are designed to give our lives direction.

As we begin to apply these lessons to our lives, we are better able to navigate the challenges we encounter every day.

As you read the examples and stories in this book, you may find that they hold a slightly different leadership application for you. Great! I hope you will apply the points in the book so that they are most useful to your situation. Those situations may range from service organizations and student groups to businesses and the workplace—or even life itself. The principles in this book can often be applied to multiple situations.

Make the decision to begin to put good leadership into practice. Not doing so would be just like hopping into that convertible and cruising in the opposite direction of where you need to be. Sure, the ride is great for a while, but eventually the time comes when you realize that the ride has led you in the wrong direction.

The ride is just as fun when you head in the right direction. So, turn the wheel and make positive changes that will help you take the lead in life and help others to do so as well.

CHAPTER 2
Finding the Motivation
CLEAR LAKE, IOWA

"Motivation is everything. You can do the work of two people, but you can't be two people. Instead, you have to inspire the next guy down the line and get him to inspire his people."

—LEE IACOCCA

I t's just a T intersection of two gravel roads in the middle of the fertile farm fields of northern Iowa. Yet it's a place people have been coming for about a half-century now, a place where people come to remember and relive moments from their past. I found my way here in a most unusual set of circumstances that began 15 years before in a high school English classroom . . .

Mr. Pearl was the kind of teacher whom students really enjoyed. Although he was a generation older than us, he was crazy enough to "fit in" yet polished enough to command respect and inspire each of us to learn and grow.

Yet as Mr. Pearl began the third quarter of this school year, he found a formidable task confronting him. He had to spend an entire quarter teaching us seniors poetry. None of us was looking forward to this boring nine weeks of class. Although we liked Mr. Pearl, even he couldn't make such a topic interesting.

Being "interesting" really wasn't the issue, though. It was the relevance of teaching this topic. Over and over again we told him that none of us read poetry. None of us ever planned to write poetry. No one planned to even study such a subject in college. Why spend time on a useless subject that in no way would help us in the future?

The first day of the third quarter arrived, and as we settled into our seats, Mr. Pearl walked to the front of the class.

"As you know, this is the day we begin our study of poetry. For the first two quarters, you have given me a lot of good reasons why you believe we should not spend one day on this topic, let alone nine weeks," he said.

At this point, he began to walk to one side of the classroom. On a table was a CD player and speakers that had not been there the previous day.

"But if you will give me just a few minutes of your time, I will try to persuade you differently," he continued.

With that, he hit the play button, and a song named "American Pie" began to play. Most of us are familiar with the chorus:

Bye, bye Miss American Pie
Drove my Chevy to the levy but the levy was dry.

The opening and closing verses of the song by Don McLean were what Mr. Pearl asked us to notice.

But February made me shiver
With every paper I delivered
Bad news on the doorstep
I couldn't take one more step.

Toward the end of the song McLean sings:

I met a girl who sang the blues
And I asked her for some happy news
But she just smiled and turned away.

Mr. Pearl explained that Don McLean was singing about the history of music in his lifetime. The first verse was about the death of Buddy Holly, Ritchie Valens, and the Big Bopper in a plane crash in Clear Lake, Iowa in February of 1959. He was a paperboy throwing on people's doorsteps the news of their deaths.

In the last verse, he sang of Janis Joplin, a talented singer who died of a drug overdose. The song was about more than music; it was about how life and lifestyles had changed in a couple of decades.

Mr. Pearl said, "Most of you ask, 'Why do we have to study poetry if none of us cares about it?' Well, I believe all of you listen to music, and as I've just shown you, music is poetry set to song. Understanding lyrics helps us to better understand the perspective of the writer. Unless none of you plans on ever listening to music, perhaps we should spend a little time learning about what you spend time listening to."

Each of us immediately recognized the importance of studying poetry. It was more than that, though. We now *wanted* to study poetry because Mr. Pearl had made the topic relevant and interesting to us!

The Incentive behind the Purpose

We opened this book by discussing destinations and the drive to reach those goals. None of that matters if you aren't motivated to even get in the car. That's why we're beginning with a look at motivation. What causes us to want to jump in the car and head toward our destination? What motivates others to also move toward that goal?

Those motivators might be labeled "incentives." Many types of incentives can drive each of us to pursue a given destination, but let's focus on four: social, economic, moral, and mental and physical wellness.

Economic incentives focus on the financial gain or loss of a decision. Does one job opportunity pay more than another? Does buying a home closer to the city cost more than one farther from town? Even if a home farther from the city is less expensive, how much more would I have to pay for gas in order to get to work? All are economic incentives.

Social incentives deal with our relationships with others. Perhaps we might have an incentive to live in a certain place because we like our neighbors. We might have an incentive to fit in and not feel left out. Mr. Pearl had given us a social incentive to study poetry. Music was important to each of us in our class. Having a better understanding of the poetry in music was a social incentive.

Moral incentives can often be summarized by the phrase "What is the right thing to do?" I could lie in order to get ahead at work or in school, but the moral incentive tells me that these actions have consequences. Our morals are often tied to lessons we learn early in life from our family, friends, and faith community.

Mental/physical wellness addresses many of our basic needs. I have an incentive to eat in order to stay well nourished. I might also face a wellness incentive that tells me not to be overweight because this will hurt me physically. I may choose one job over another because of the work environment. Perhaps one career offers flexible scheduling, which takes some of the stress out of our hectic schedule and provides mental wellness.

For any given destination in our lives, one or more incentives are usually in place. For instance, I enjoy the part of my career that allows me to speak to groups. What is my incentive to do this type of work? I do get paid for the job, so I have an economic incentive. I enjoy meeting and working with others, so the social incentive is present. The work is exciting to me and provides mental wellness, too.

If we choose our career only because of the economic incentive, we will constantly move to new jobs that pay a higher salary. There is certainly nothing wrong with making more money, but many research studies show that salary is not the most important factor in whether a person accepts a job or stays with a business.

The workplace environment can be very important. Maybe the business allows its employees to work from home so that parents can spend more time with their children. In these cases, social and moral incentives may be at work.

A major airline hires many reservation agents who take calls from their own homes. This arrangement was popular with housewives, who were able to earn extra income yet were able to continue to devote time to their homes and families. This airline was able to provide an economic incentive for these agents through the salary it paid them, but more important, the social, moral, and mental/physical wellness incentives were also at work.

Working from home may take some of the stress out of juggling work and home, thus creating a mental wellness incentive. This may translate into an economic incentive because staying healthy and having less stress should mean less health care expense. Almost every situation in life is composed of several incentives. These incentives should help us find the underlying purpose in what we do each day.

Finding destinations that meet several of these incentives is a good thing. Incentives can affect us in the short term, long term, or both. Looking at the big picture is important, not just moving toward the incentive that offers the most immediate gratification.

Later in this book we will discuss the challenge we face when incentives tell us to do two different things at the same time. These are often issues of integrity, and they shape who we are as leaders. For now, though, we are simply focusing on positive incentives in one's life.

Finding Purpose in What We Do

Each of us has been in a classroom before and wondered to ourselves, "When am I ever going to use what they are teaching me?" If we don't see a reason to use it in life, we will probably not be very interested in investing our time in studying the subject. The same can be said for the mission of any group. If people don't see much reason to invest time in advancing the mission, they are less likely to be motivated to join or become active in the group.

Mr. Pearl was a master at helping classes to find the purpose in an assignment. Understanding and using this skill in business and life are critical. These are some of the most important leadership qualities we can put to use.

In 2006 the Bill and Melinda Gates Foundation commissioned a study to determine why students drop out of high school. They found that more than six in 10 of the dropouts had grade-point averages that were a C or better. Most students were not dropping out because they were failing classes; they left school because they had become disconnected with the purpose of school in their lives. A majority cited that they would have worked harder if expectations for the quality of their work were higher. Many of these students needed to find purpose in their schoolwork and relevance to their life and future.

Understanding the purpose behind what we do is critical to individual and group success. Whenever I teach motivation and goal setting, I like to discuss the "Rules for Scooping Manure." This comes from several years of hands-on research I have gained while working on our farm. To my knowledge, no university researchers have tackled this subject. However, I firmly believe that if someone can be motivated to scoop manure, the steps involved in doing so should have application in motivating us to do less daunting (and less smelly) tasks in life.

During the course of a year, hundreds of cattle will be received at our farm. Before these calves are sent out to pasture, they must be sent through a chute to receive all of their vaccinations. Just as a baby is inoculated against certain diseases, a calf needs certain shots and boosters to keep it safe from bovine threats.

One of the by-products of moving cattle into pens and through the chute is the manure that is generated. My experience with that manure has led me to the following points that are necessary in motivating groups. I call these "Rules for Scooping Manure." In this chapter we will tackle only point number one. The rest of the points will be discussed in later chapters.

RULES FOR SCOOPING MANURE

1. The *purpose* for scooping must be well established.
2. *Everyone* should have to take a turn scooping.
3. *Enthusiasm* is critical in creating the best working environment.
4. Developing a *system* makes for efficient and effective work.
5. Sincere *compliments* lay the foundation for future successes.

Let me be quite frank. If you have no reason to scoop manure, you will not scoop it merely for enjoyment. The *purpose* of scooping must be well established.

Why do I help scoop manure? Because I've seen what happens when you don't scoop the manure. If the manure is not cleaned from the pens and chute regularly, the concrete floor becomes slick. People and cattle begin to slip and fall. The manure begins to build up around the metal posts and gates, where its acidity will eat through the metal and cause it to rust. If allowed to accumulate, the manure not only begins to create a very noticeable odor but also attracts lots of flies. Manure needs to be scooped for many reasons.

Because I and those who work on our farm know the *purpose* of scooping the manure, we are willing to regularly perform the task. We know the consequences of not performing the job.

Although manure scooping and my example of Mr. Pearl's poetry teaching seem far removed from each other, both have the same root: in order to motivate people to action, we first have to clearly understand the purpose behind what is to be done. Second, we have to understand the benefits of taking time to complete the task. Finally, the task has to be relevant to our lives.

Some people in your group will buy into the mission more than others, but they must see some purpose in the mission; otherwise, they will never take the time to begin to complete the task, let alone scoop manure.

The First and Only Rule of Motivation

I appreciate leadership author John Maxwell's definition of leadership: "Leadership *is* influence." That influence can move people in positive and negative directions. But make no doubt about it: each of us is a leader because each of us influences others. We are also influenced by others, but for now let's talk about the influence we have and how we can use it to positively affect others.

Leadership's influence begins with an environment that facilitates growth. Let's go back to Mr. Pearl's classroom. It was a place we wanted to be. He made learning fun. He genuinely cared about each student. The environment was right for leadership and learning to take place.

Leadership requires a good environment for growth. I cannot overstate the importance of creating the right environment for maximum positive influence to take place.

I once served as a trainer at a summer leadership camp. One particular week each year was designated as "public speaking week." This was a time when normal leadership sessions were designed to help students work on their communication skills.

On this particular week, a soon-to-be freshman in high school, Matt, came to the camp. It was his first time away from home, and he was shy and reluctant to get involved. Although he wanted to learn to become a better public speaker, he had little prior experience. One of the main reasons he was motivated to come to the camp was because other recreation opportunities such as swimming and sports were offered. He wouldn't have to spend his entire time learning to speak.

One of the first assignments at the camp was to break into small groups. Matt happened to be one of six students in the group led by me. The assignment was simple. "Stand in front of the group and speak for two to three minutes about someone you admire."

One by one each student stood and delivered a short talk about a role model in his or her life. Finally, it was Matt's turn. He had waited until the very end, and I could tell he was really nervous.

I cheerfully coaxed him, "Matt, we're ready to hear what you've got for us."

He said nothing and simply stared at the ground and shook his head.

What was I to do? If he didn't participate at all during the week, he might go home with a very negative feeling about camp. The situation could go either way, and I needed to turn it into a positive influence rather than a negative experience.

I didn't know exactly what to say that would suddenly inspire him to speak, but I had to say something.

"Well, Matt, I bet you've got someone you could tell us about. You don't have to speak very long; just give us a few sentences about a person you look up to," I said, hoping to muster a response from him.

"I can't think of anybody," he mumbled, still too petrified to look at me or anyone else in the group.

There had to be a way to break through to him. How could I attempt to create an environment where he would begin to share?

"How about someone in your family, Matt? Maybe a teacher? How about a friend? It could even be someone you've never met before."

Each query was met with a soft "no" spoken toward the ground.

"Don't worry about it, Matt. Just take a minute and see if you can think of someone. You really don't even need to say much about the person, just give us a name and a sentence about him or her," I offered, hoping to nudge him into saying something more.

"I guess I admire myself," he finally said, looking up from the ground.

"Yourself? Great! Why do you admire yourself, Matt?"

"I work hard."

"You work hard? What do you do?" I countered.

"I load hay in the summer," he said.

I know how tough it is to buck bales in the summer. The bales are heavy, and the temperatures are sweltering. But for the moment, I was going to act as if I knew nothing about the job.

"Why is it so tough?" I asked.

"Well, the bales are heavy, and we work all day," he explained.

I'm sure the job was difficult for him. He was not a very big guy, and I'm sure it was all he could do to lift the big bales. From this point, we began to talk about hauling hay. Each of his answers grew in length, and he slowly began to make more eye contact with me than with the ground at his feet. All the while, he remained seated at the picnic table in the middle of our group.

Two days later, this same small group got together once again. The assignment was to talk about the same person as you had earlier, but now, using the skills you had learned during the week, you were to improve upon your earlier talk.

Once again Matt waited until the very end to speak.

"Are you ready, Matt?"

Something amazing happened. He stood.

That was a very big deal. This was a student who was petrified to speak just two days ago. As he stood, he still placed one hand on the picnic table, a visible link to something stable. The table represented something that gave him comfort, yet now he was standing and speaking. Maybe it was just for 30 seconds, but that was quite an accomplishment.

I must admit that I somewhat stumbled into getting Matt to speak. I didn't know how things would turn out, but I did know that I had to get him to a comfortable and safe environment before he would ever decide it was all right for him to speak.

Matt believed in the purpose of the camp. He knew that public speaking was something important for him to learn. But his fears were keeping him from seeing the original reason for achieving his goal. He first had to have a safe environment in which to learn and grow before he would move toward accomplishing even the smallest step.

Remember our discussion of incentives. Two social incentives might be at work simultaneously. Matt knew he needed to work on his public speaking skills so that he could better interact with others. We all feel a strong social incentive to feel included. However, a social incentive also drives us not to embarrass ourselves in front of others.

Perhaps Matt felt both of these incentives pulling him in different directions. Only when he felt that he was in a safe environment could he move forward. The group was not there to make fun of him or to make him feel embarrassed. The group was there to support him. It is important to take into account the different incentives at work in such situations.

Creating the Right Environment

I serve on the board of a hospital and speak at many health-care-related events. Over time I've seen my share of medical facilities. If you've ever been to a children's hospital, you've probably noticed that it has a totally different look from most other facilities.

The rooms and hallways are painted a variety of bright colors. Cartoon characters are often painted on the walls as well. Doctors and nurses wear fun ties and coats. The patients may receive toys to play with. The entire atmosphere attempts to take what can be a scary place and turn it into something fun.

Most other hospitals are not this way. They may look very nice, and the staff may be very professional, but it's just another medical facility. Just because the patients may be older doesn't mean that they don't have fears about going to the hospital.

I was once speaking for the directors of a major hospital. They had just completed an extensive survey of hundreds of patients over the course of several months. They wanted to learn what they needed to do to better their performance.

After displaying several charts with statistics and customer satisfaction scores, the director of the study said, "We can sum up the entire survey in one sentence. People cared more about how we treated them than about how we treated their illness."

Sure, these people wanted to get well, but their perception of how they got well was influenced mostly by how the doctors and nurses treated them. If they were surrounded by upbeat and friendly people who took extra time to help them and their families understand what would be happening, the scores went up. Recovery times were quicker. People felt better about the process.

What job we have or what meeting we are going to lead is not what matters; we must think about the environment. My wife teaches Spanish to students in kindergarten through fifth grade. I love going to her room. Sombreros hang from the ceiling, and Latin musical instruments sit on the tables. The room is filled with fun posters and lots of colorful piñatas. My wife constantly has to tell me to quit trying on the sombreros every time I show up. It's a fun place.

Many of us think that once we are an adult we can no longer have fun. Don't go overboard, but think of little things you can do to create an environment where people want to be. Maybe you just play some music as people are coming to the meeting. Maybe you put a few fun posters on the wall. At the John Deere Harvester Works in Moline, Illinois, the seats for visiting groups are seats out of combines. Add life to life itself, whether at home or at work.

Think about what you do and how you can make the work space or meeting space a place where people want to be. We are not creating a giant playroom, but people must feel comfortable with their environment before they will push toward their goals.

Remember our Mustang example from the opening of the book. If the car is stripped on the inside, the top is broken and won't come down, I don't have air conditioning on a sweltering day, and a barking Chihuahua is in the seat next to me, the environment is not conducive to me driving the car for long! Create the environment that will facilitate growth.

The Achievement Model

Think of a climbing team that is headed to the peak of a very tall mountain. We begin at the base camp, an area we'll label as the "green zone." Here at the base camp the altitude is such that no one requires additional oxygen. We still enjoy many of the conveniences of home, such as stores where climbers can buy supplies and gear and communication links to the rest of the world. The green zone is a gathering place for those who are ready to climb the mountain.

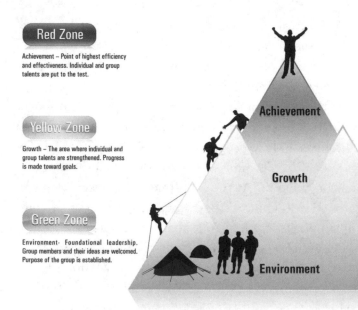

Red Zone

Achievement – Point of highest efficiency and effectiveness. Individual and group talents are put to the test.

Yellow Zone

Growth – The area where individual and group talents are strengthened. Progress is made toward goals.

Green Zone

Environment· Foundational leadership. Group members and their ideas are welcomed. Purpose of the group is established.

This green zone represents our comfort zone. The climb cannot begin without going here first. One of the biggest mistakes leaders make in trying to motivate individuals and groups to action is that they skip the base camp and immediately try to move the entire team halfway up the mountain. It's a sure way to lose half of your climbers. Why? The team has not had time to acclimate itself to the climate and the mission that lies ahead. Developing the right environment is key.

My wife and I once took an overland journey from Chile to Bolivia. The border of these two countries lies along the Andes Mountains. For two nights we stayed at camps high in the mountains. In fact, for most of 48 hours we were at an altitude of more than 14,000 feet.

For people like us who do not live at an altitude anywhere close to two and a half miles above sea level, we noticed the lack of oxygen. In fact, many of us had a dull headache for two days. Once we descended a couple thousand feet, the headache immediately went away.

Because we were not acclimated to living at a high altitude, our quick ascent to that level only gave us headaches. Likewise, if we quickly skip the green zone stage of leadership development, we will create a lot of headaches.

So how do you get the group to the green zone in the first place? There is not a one-size-fits-all formula for making it happen. It requires time and effort by the leadership. Mr. Pearl did not attend a class where he was told that in order to teach poetry to seniors in high school, you should use the song "American Pie" to motivate them. Yet, that is what he did because he understood that if we were ever going to move to the "growth" and "achievement" portions of the mountain model, he had to get us fully in the green zone first.

Mr. Pearl first established the **purpose** for studying poetry. Next, he put himself back in a student's desk and looked at the world from the eyes of a 17-year-old. He was able to move us to the green zone by using music as the catalyst for learning. He created the right **environment**. Music was something with which each of us was comfortable. It was a comfortable beginning, or base camp, for our study of poetry.

The motivational process is certainly lined with challenges. Don't be discouraged. Getting to know a group and beginning the leadership process takes time.

I was once facilitating a leadership conference for high school juniors and seniors in Iowa. Two hundred students were attending a 24-hour conference that went from noon Saturday to noon Sunday.

The last activity of the evening was called "Thank You for Making a Difference." Each student wrote a letter to someone who had made a difference in his or her life. The students often wrote to a parent, a teacher, or another role model in their community who had helped them come to this conference. The letters did not have to be long, but each student needed to simply show appreciation for the person taking time to help him or her.

This is always a great activity to conclude the evening. It helps everyone realize the importance of others and reflect on what he or she can do to help others in the same way. On this evening, everyone began writing his or her letters just as planned. However, I noticed that one young man, Nathan, was not writing a letter. I could see that his paper was blank and he was simply staring at the ceiling.

He was sitting next to two of his friends, and I knew that if he didn't get to work, he would soon bother them and distract them from writing their letters. So, I knew that I needed to go and get Nathan back on task.

I didn't want to call him out in front of everyone, so I simply knelt beside his chair and said, "Nathan, are you having trouble writing your letter?"

"I don't want to write a letter," he said as he continued to stare at the ceiling.

"Well, Nathan, you don't have to write a long letter, but it is important that you write a letter to someone who has helped you," I replied.

"I don't have anyone to write to," he countered.

"Yeah, I know it can sometimes be tough to think of whom you want to write to, but I bet we can come up with someone to say thank you to," I explained. "Could you write to someone in your family?"

"Nope," came the quick reply.

"How about a friend?"

"Nope," he countered once again.

"Maybe you could write to a teacher," I offered.

"Nope."

"Nathan, you don't even have to know this person. It could be a sports star or TV personality. We'll find the person's address and send him or her the letter."

"Nope," came the reply once again.

By now I realized that no matter what suggestion I offered, it would be met with a quick "nope." I was frustrated that Nathan did not appreciate the importance of saying "thanks" to others who were active in his life.

"Nathan, look around the room for a moment," I said. "Everyone else in the room is writing a letter. It doesn't have to be a long letter. It can be two or three sentences, but you must write a letter before you can leave this evening."

Nathan was frustrated as well, realizing that his "nope" was not going to satisfy me. "I'll just write to you, then," he said.

This is not the result I had intended, but perhaps it was making the best of a bad situation. At least he would be spending time writing a letter and would not have the time to bother others who were quietly working. If he wanted to write to me, at least he would be doing something instead of just sitting and staring at the ceiling.

As students finished their letters, we would stamp them and mail them, or they could agree to hand deliver them when they saw that person at home. I saw Nathan slop down three or four sentences and fold his letter. He walked to the front of the room and handed it to me.

The letter had my name on it, so there was no reason to stamp it. Once all of the students had left the room, I opened it to see what Nathan had written to me. The letter read:

Dear Mr. McCrea,

I am sorry I could not complete your assignment. As I look outside and see the beautiful trees, I'm reminded of the walks I used to take through the woods with my grandmother. I came to this conference last year and should have written to her, but now I can't because she passed away. I'm sorry I could not complete your assignment.

Nathan

My assignment had certainly not gone as planned. What I had viewed as disinterest had in fact been Nathan's way of reflecting upon the importance of his grandmother in his life. Without a way to write to her, he was simply reflecting upon those memories as he stared at the ceiling.

Notice that I had created the right environment for most of the people at the conference. I was playing reflective music, and my instructions got everyone else in the room in the right mind-set to write a letter. However, creating the right environment to learn and achieve is a two-way street. We have to take into account the needs of those with whom we are working. This takes time. We have to go out of our way to better know those with whom we work.

The Green Zone

Don't be discouraged at the time and effort it takes to build the right environment and create a strong green zone. I once interviewed Canadian mountain climber Alan Hobson, who made three attempts to climb Mount Everest and finally reached the peak on his third climb. I asked him about the preparation for an Everest expedition. Most groups will take three to seven years to raise the capital and prepare mentally and physically for the climb.

He noted, "If there is one thing that concerns me today, it is that there are people who have not taken the small steps and want to take a giant leap to Mount Everest, and often the result of that can be fatal." Whether it is a real-life ascent of Everest or a figurative climb for us to achieve our goals, we need to take the time to prepare in the green zone. Preparing ourselves and others for the task ahead takes time.

Franklin Delano Roosevelt had the makings of a man who could have been completely out of touch with the vast majority of

Americans. He was related to eleven former presidents, either by birth or through marriage. His family was wealthy and he had always lived in a fine home. During his youth, he took vacations to Europe and attended the best schools.

It may have been an event in 1921 though, that most influenced his life and future presidency. He contracted polio, a disease that at the age of thirty-nine rendered his legs and hips paralyzed. His wife Eleanor saw how the challenge was actually preparing him for what lay ahead. "I know that he had real fear when he was first taken ill, but he learned to surmount it. After that I never heard him say he was afraid of anything," she said. In 1932 Franklin Delano Roosevelt was elected president and he quickly worked to restore confidence in the country during the Great Depression.

Franklin Roosevelt once said, "The test of our progress is not whether we add more to the abundance of those who have much; it is whether we provide enough for those who have too little." He understood fear and he had learned to overcome it. His ability to not only relate to the needs of others but, most importantly, to help fill those needs and ease their fears, is why FDR is often regarded as one of the nation's best presidents. FDR understood that leadership begins in the green zone!

During the Great Depression people feared what might happen to their children. They feared they might not have a job, or even be able to get a job. FDR began "fireside chats," with the first delivered over the radio on Sunday evening, March 12, 1933. Many Americans still refer to those broadcasts as if the president had sat down in their own living room simply to talk and reassure them about the future.

Motivation and Purpose for Life

I was a student who was convinced that poetry had no purpose in my life. Mr. Pearl did such a good job of creating motivation and purpose behind this "useless" subject that now, 15 years after that class, I had driven to the T intersection of two gravel roads in the middle of the fertile farm fields of northern Iowa. This is the place where Don McLean said the music died.

I sat down with a farmer named Jeff, who owns the field today. The plane carrying Buddy Holly crashed on his farm. Holly and friends had just played a concert at the Surf Ballroom in Clear Lake and then boarded a plane to fly to their next stop. Ritchie Valens didn't have a seat on the plane but wanted to make the trip. He and Waylon Jennings had a coin flip to see who would get the last seat, and Valens won. The flight lasted only three minutes before it crashed just beyond the intersection of these gravel roads. Today a small memorial marks the spot of the crash.

Jeff says, "Virtually every time I come to this farm, there will be a car or two parked here. People will walk out from the road out to the crash site, arm in arm, in total silence. It's the place where the music died." As Don McLean wrote in his song "American Pie," "Something touched me deep inside the day the music died." It touched a generation of Americans who still drive to see the Surf Ballroom and pay their respects at the memorial in Jeff's field.

The song's lyrics touched me, too. However, I would never have known the significance of those words if I hadn't understood that music was poetry set to song. Mr. Pearl was the one who showed me the purpose behind the study of the subject. I was in turn motivated to learn more about not only poetry but also Buddy Holly and his final concert at the Surf.

Our ability to help others find purpose and motivation is critical to our ability to lead. When done well, it led me to drive to Clear Lake, Iowa, to better understand the poetry I had read. It can lead others toward goals with an even deeper purpose in life.

CHAPTER 3
How Groups Grow
CHICAGO, ILLINOIS

"Let him who would move the world first move himself."

—SOCRATES

I was in Chicago for a speaking engagement, and because it was during the weekend, I decided to stay an extra day and see my good friend Corey. He invited me to go to church with him, and what resulted was not only an interesting story but also a classic study in recruitment and retention.

I'd always heard a lot about Salem Baptist Church. Its membership tops 20,000, making the church congregation three times the population of my county! When a church is three times the size of where you grew up, you're bound to experience culture shock. Perhaps Corey expected this.

"You know, Drew, Salem is going to be different from what you've seen before," he explained as we drove down the streets of the South Side of Chicago on our way to an evening service.

"We're going to move, we're going to clap, we're going to sing. You'd probably say we're going to 'get down,'" he continued in his description of the place.

I simply nodded my head and thought to myself, "I'm sure it will be a little different, but I'm well traveled; I'm sure it won't be that hard to adjust."

We arrived early, and Corey found a seat for me in the fourth pew from the front. He sang in the choir, so he walked behind the pulpit to take his seat there. Now with the crowd filling in around me, the service was ready to begin.

I should have known that I was in trouble when the two ladies in front of me reached in their purses to get their own tambourines they had brought with them to service. We were ready to get down!

I stood, clapped, sang, and danced. I did everything that a white farm kid could to keep up with 18,000 parishioners who found this commonplace. The church was so large it had video cameras that flashed images up on giant screens in front of the audience. As I looked above me and saw a similar face on the screen, I thought, "Well, there's another white guy here!" Then I realized it was me!

Let me pause the story here for a moment. I mention the outward differences in appearance in this story for an important reason. Barriers usually exist, whether real or perceived, to anyone becoming part of a new group. My friend Corey is black and grew up in the city of Chicago. I, on the other hand, am a white farm boy from northwest Missouri. Remember that mountains are sometimes molehills in disguise. We must take steps to see our perceived barriers in a new light if we are to reach the summit.

Was it really that unusual for me to have thoughts like, "I wonder what people think of me?" running through my mind. On the outside, it would be easy for me to be perceived as different, as someone who didn't quite fit in.

Remember our mountain climbing model of achievement. Leadership begins in the green zone, which is influenced by the environment we create. Even though people might see the same purpose and relevance in becoming members of a group, they could easily say to themselves, "I want to climb this mountain, but I don't want to climb it with them."

It is much like the story of the little boy in Sunday school who was asked by his teacher whether he wanted to go to heaven someday. All of the boys and girls in the class raised their hands except for this one little boy.

The teacher asked, "Tim, why don't you want to go to heaven?"

He replied, "Well, it won't be any fun if all of them are there, too!"

The preceding chapter spoke of the importance of creating the right environment, or green zone, as a foundation for future growth and achievement. The green zone must not only build the right environment but also establish a shared purpose and motivate people toward achieving goals.

This chapter continues to focus on the green zone, but it addresses topics of recruitment and retention. People are motivated to join a group or stay with a company because they see its purpose or relevance in their lives. Even when we share a similar purpose, though, what influences people to join us in the pursuit of that goal?

Recruitment Inside Out

Race is something we see on the outside, yet on the inside, we have just as many barriers to joining and becoming active in groups. Will people like me? Will this group help me? Is spending time to be a part of this worth it? Each of us must answer many questions before becoming involved in a group.

After one hour of singing, Corey came down from the choir and took a seat beside me. I whispered, "So how did I do?"

He smiled and said, "You really stand out here."

Toward the end of the service, as Reverend Meeks concluded his message, something interesting happened. "If there is anyone here tonight who would like to be a part of Salem, I invite them to come on down now," he said, his voice filled with a bit of a rumble, the type

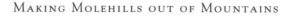

of voice one would expect from a pastor who had just delivered a moving dissertation of the application of the Bible in one's life.

Some people began to come forward. At this point, a gentleman next to me reached over and tapped me on the knee. He seemed like a nice fellow, but we didn't know each other. We said "hello" when he sat down next to me, but that was it. **He had no reason to talk to me. He could clearly see that Corey and I were friends because the two of us were visiting.**

"If you'd like to go down, well, I'd be glad to walk down with you so you didn't have to walk alone," he offered.

The story goes far beyond church and faith. It cuts right to the heart of motivation, recruitment, and retention. I'm sure this man wasn't thinking about all of that, but he was a master at it, and he didn't even realize it. Leadership requires people to go out of their way to interact with others, especially when it comes to the area of recruitment.

Where Recruitment Begins: Names

What follows may seem so simple that it is ridiculous to include it in this book. Yet what I am about to share is so important and rarely mastered. Your ability to do the following will instantly help you "connect" with people. Simply use their names.

John is a gentleman in his 70s who has an interesting habit when it comes to using people's names. He is a friend of mine, and whenever he eats at a fast-food restaurant, he reads the name tag of the person taking his order and then smiles and calls the person by name.

One day I was standing with him in a very long line, and we were waiting to place our order. The long wait made everyone difficult to get along with. When John finally made it to the head of the line, instead of just quickly giving his order so he could get served, he smiled and said, "Hi, Tiffany!" He had never met this young lady. He just read her name off of her badge. He isn't sarcastic, just polite. You would be amazed at the smiles he gets in return and the great service he receives.

John later explained to me the importance of a person's name to that individual. As Dale Carnegie once said, a person's name is the "sweetest and most important sound" to him or her. If a name is on a name tag, reading it and saying it are pretty easy things to do. But what if a person isn't wearing a name tag? More important, how do you remember that name for days, weeks, or even years after you meet the person?

Using people's names is the first step in creating a welcoming environment. A school district in Houston, Texas, recently took time to train its school bus drivers on how to help students succeed in the classroom. This may sound odd because the drivers don't actually teach any students; they just pick them up in the morning and drop them off in the afternoon.

However, the school district knew the importance of helping students have a good start to their day. This began with each bus driver using the students' names when they got on and off of the bus. Drivers also tried to learn a little about each student who rode their route. If a driver knew David liked the Dallas Cowboys, he or she might ask him something about football.

The cliché "People don't care how much you know until they know how much you care" is very true. In this school district, it began with the school bus drivers helping the students get a good start to their day.

My wife teaches Spanish at an elementary school. Her school district also knows the importance of building the right environment for a student to learn and grow. When a student gets to school each morning, the teachers have a goal for all students to be greeted by name at least three times before they enter their classroom.

This means that teachers greet students when they get off the bus. Other teachers greet students when they enter the school.

Classroom teachers stand at their doors and welcome each student to class each morning.

Businesses are more successful when employees greet customers by name. For many years I was a loyal customer of a dry cleaner in a nearby town. The cleaners did a good job of cleaning my clothes, but what I really appreciated about the shop was the owner. Every time I walked in the door, he would great me by name. He would also take a moment to visit with me. His conversation was brief, yet it made me feel like the most important customer he had. I know many others who went to the same dry cleaner and shared similar experiences.

Not only are using names and building the right environment important for school students or dry cleaning customers, but also these actions are critical at all stages of life. You may say, "My group or business is so large that there is no way I can ever remember everyone's name." My wife sees more than 600 students each week at her school, yet she eventually learns each student's name.

Rarely do I meet someone who says he or she is great at remembering names. For most of us, this is a skill we must develop. How many times have you met someone and five seconds later you can't recall his or her name? This happens to all of us. Such an event is not a memory problem. Any one of us could remember a person's name for 10 seconds if we knew we absolutely needed to remember it.

The "if" in that sentence is key. Most of us don't think about remembering someone's name until it is too late. One approach I adopted when meeting several new people was to say to myself, "Andrew, pay attention. You are ready to meet several people, so concentrate on their names." Sounds silly but it helps your mind prepare for the exercise that is about to begin.

Then, as you meet each person, silently repeat the names of the people you have previously met. I might just be standing in the room, but I will begin to look around the room and repeat the names of each person to myself as I see him or her. Repetition is an important key.

Let's turn the name game around for just a second. No one is perfect at remembering names. Even though you may have met a person on several occasions, if you are not a familiar acquaintance, the other person may not recall your name.

How many times have you heard someone ask, "Do you remember who I am?" We are putting the other person on the defensive when we say this. If the other person doesn't remember our name, he or she feels bad because we obviously hoped we would be remembered. The person ends up having to apologize because he or she can't remember. It's definitely not a good way to begin a conversation.

Never assume a person remembers you. Instead, say, "Hi, I'm Andrew McCrea. We met briefly at the leadership conference in Columbia." Whether or not the other person remembers you, this person can say, "Yes, Andrew, it is great to see you again."

Remember that when we work in the green zone, we are working to build an environment where leadership can thrive. This begins by helping people feel good about themselves when we use their names and not making them feel bad when they forget ours. It's not about us; it's about them.

Why People Decide to Stay

What makes people decide to join a group? Using names is a start, but we must build on this solid beginning. A combination of little things often influences people to join and become active in a group. Conversely, several little negative things are what push them into inactivity or cause them never to join.

We've been discussing these little things that make a big difference. Names are one of them, but this technique requires a proactive approach when interacting with others. Let me give you another success story, another example of a seemingly insignificant thing that can make a big difference.

At most churches, traditionally, after the service is complete, the minister or priest will stand at the door and greet people as they leave. There is certainly nothing wrong with this, but what might a more proactive approach look like? What might be the differences of using this approach?

I knew a small-town minister who had two churches for which he was responsible. Every Sunday morning he would preach in one church, and then, upon the completion of that service, he would drive a few miles to the other country church and deliver the service to that group of parishioners. With such a tight time schedule, he could have several excuses for why he couldn't take time to greet and visit with people at either church.

He didn't see it that way, though. Fifteen minutes before the service began at each church, he would quietly go to each pew in the church. He would greet and shake hands with every single person in the church. It didn't matter whether someone had been coming to the church for 50 years or whether he or she was visiting for the first time; every person was greeted. The greeting was polite and sincere. No one ever got the feeling that he or she was being "recruited." This minister just had a way of going to the people instead of them "having" to walk by him on their way out of the church at the con-clusion of the services.

What was the result? Within a couple of years of the minister being at the church, attendance was up by about 50%. Certainly, sev-eral factors were at work, but parishioners would tell you that a lot had to do with the minister's proactive approach when it came to working with people.

This chapter opened with the story of my trip to Salem Baptist Church. I have attended the church on subsequent trips to Chicago.

Every time I go there, I have a number of people come and welcome me. They are polite, not forceful. They seem very sincere. It is part of the culture there.

Salem began with a congregation of just over 100 members. In 20 years the congregation approached 20,000! Little things add up. Building the environment for growth can make amazing things happen for your group, organization, or business.

Just as the small-town minister or Salem Baptist Church experienced positive results, the opposite approach will have people fleeing your group. In college I was a part of a campus-wide leadership group. You had to interview to be a part of the organization, and I was glad to be selected to be a member my freshman year. I participated in several events that worked to further the university and its students.

During the middle of my junior year, I left college when I was elected to a national office in another student organization. This was a great opportunity to travel the country and work in many leadership roles, but it did require me to leave my studies for two semesters. When I returned to the university, I attended a meeting of that leadership group that I had joined my freshman year.

During the time I was gone, all of the officers had graduated, and the group had entirely new leadership. I knew only one of the officers and one other member. The goals of the organization had changed. The fundraiser for the group was to do singing telegrams (it didn't matter whether I could sing or not; I just didn't think this was the kind of thing that was helping us move toward our mission).

None of the new officers cared to talk with me or welcome me back to the group. After a couple of meetings, I lost interest in being a part of the group. In the following years, I understood that the organization struggled to live up to what it had once been. I believe it happened because the leadership was no longer interested in getting its membership to the green zone.

Not only had the environment eroded in this group, but also the group had lost its mission and purpose. Members no longer saw the relevance of the group's work to their own goals for campus life.

The same can be said for those in business. When stores, companies, or even individual proprietors forget the importance of how they treat customers, those customers soon grow dissatisfied and leave.

No matter our destination in life, the environment we create will do much to influence our success. It even applies to those who have goals like that of Alan Hobson, who made three attempts to climb Mount Everest. Consider this:

> Tenzing Norgay, the Sherpa climber who, along with Sir Edmund Hillary, was the first man to reach the summit of Mount Everest, knew how important green zone activities were to the entire mission. He said, "You cannot be a good mountaineer, however great your ability, unless you are cheerful and have the spirit of comradeship. Friends are as important as achievement." Reducing a mountainous goal to a molehill requires a spirit that reaches out to others and helps them be comfortable with the climb.

Changing Our Point of View

The three key components to creating a green zone that recruits and retains members are as follows:

1. Attitude. Are we like the gentleman who sat next to me at Salem Baptist Church? Are we friendly and welcoming? Realize that attitude should be active rather than passive. We must go out of our way to create the right environment for future growth and achievement.

2. Purpose. It doesn't matter how good I feel about myself or the group. If I don't see a purpose, I probably won't stick around for long.

3. Perspective. Can we lead the group while still seeing the situation through the group members' eyes?

Consider the importance of perspective. Do we simply see the world from our own point of view without taking into account the views of others? There was once an owner of a large Midwestern department store who personally interviewed candidates who applied for management positions in his store. He conducted a formal interview and then took the potential employees out to eat. Although the job candidates didn't know it, the meal was an important part of the interview as well.

The department store owner noticed how people ate. He especially noticed if they salted their food. If they salted their food before tasting it, he would not hire them. He said it showed that the candidates were resistant to change and too impatient. If they already had their mind made up to salt their food without tasting it, they would likely be intolerant of others' ideas without listening to them.

Take a look at the following picture. Can you guess where this picture was taken? Two parts of this picture seem like they don't go together. In the foreground we see cactuses, which are usually an indication of a hot and dry climate. Yet in the background we see what appear to be a sheet of ice and snow-capped mountains.

If you show this picture to people in South America, many can quickly tell you the location of this place. The photo comes from the Salar de Uyuni, a giant salt flat in Bolivia. What appears to be ice is actually salt. The area can be hot and dry, which is why cactuses are growing there. However, the surrounding mountain peaks rise over 16,000 feet, which is why they are covered with snow.

Where was this picture taken?

Most people can't identify the photograph because they have never been in a place that combined such geographical features. Each of us has to take time to better understand the world and the people around us. The most dangerous viewpoint is for us to "assume that we know" something. This leads us to make decisions not based on fact.

Perceptions, Assumptions, and Integrity

The man was intriguing. Put him in the middle of farm country and he might blend in a little bit, but in the departure lounge of a flight bound for Salt Lake City, he conspicuously stood out. People tried not to stare, but you could tell the same question was on everybody's mind: "Why and where was this man flying?"

He wore the traditional black broad-rimmed hat, black coat, and suspenders of an old order Amish farmer and looked to be in his mid-70s. I thought we might have acquaintances in common, since I have Amish friends who do blacksmith work for us. Although the Amish do travel, sometimes taking long trips across the country to see relatives, it certainly was rare to see such a gentlemen in an airport. I wondered if perhaps he was flying to meet some of his family, or perhaps there was another reason. It wasn't any of my business, but I was curious.

As I settled into my seat, this very man stopped at my aisle and took the seat next to me. We exchanged hellos, after which I opened up the conversation with, "So where are you headed today? Are you stopping in Salt Lake or heading somewhere else?" I didn't figure I was being too nosy; most travelers exchange such information.

He smiled and with a soft voice said, "Well, I've got a big trip ahead of me."

"Oh really?" I countered with a raised eyebrow. "Ya headed to the west coast?"

"No, a little farther than that . . . I'm headed to China."

China? Was he pulling my leg? Why in the world would this man be headed to China? Was it the vacation he'd always dreamed of? "Wow, that's a long trip," I responded. "Is that a place you've always dreamed of visiting?"

"Oh, this is my eighth trip," he stated with a grin. "I'm going for business."

I consider myself a well-worn traveler, but eight trips to China? What on earth could be the reason an Amish gentlemen would need to visit China so frequently? Was he an entrepreneur using the Amish as a guise to get the inside track on a big deal?

"You see, in my community we don't use electricity," he explained, unsure of whether I knew much about the Amish way of life. "I run a store in our community that sells oil lamps, but no one in this country makes them anymore. That's why I go to China . . . to visit the factories that make them and then place an order for what we will need for the next two or three years."

As we continued our conversation, I reflected on how much my perception of the situation was changing. It is human nature to look at the outward situation and make a judgment on what is before us. I'd figured this Amish man was probably making his first flight when in reality he had already traveled seven times to a nation most people never see.

Our perceptions and assumptions are never a substitute for fact and reality. We will tend to look at each situation in the context of what we already know. If we continue to do this, our assumptions lead us to incorrect conclusions.

Assumptions and false information lead us to make poor decisions. Let's look back at the reports of the first airplane flight at Kitty Hawk, North Carolina. The news was hard to believe. A telegram had just arrived at the Wright family's home on December 17, 1903. The message from Orville to his parents read as follows:

```
176 C KA CS 33 Paid. Via Norfolk Va
Kitty Hawk N C Dec 17
Bishop M Wright
      7 Hawthorne St
Success four flights thursday morning all against twenty one mile
wind started from Level with engine power alone average speed
through air thirty one mile longest 57 seconds inform Press
home Christmas.    Orevelle Wright 525P
```

The telegram contained a couple of errors, including the spelling of Orville's name and the correct length of the longest flight (59 seconds instead of 57). Yet the message proclaimed the news of the first successful flight of an airplane, a message that, ironically, few newspapers were interested in printing. Even the Wrights' hometown paper in Dayton snubbed the story as unworthy since the craft had only been in the air for 59 seconds, if in fact it had even accomplished that.

Only the telegraph operator in Kitty Hawk found the story of interest, and he relayed it to his friend, Harry P. Moore of the *Norfolk Virginian Pilot*. That paper was the first to run a story about the flight. Moore, who was not present for the flight and had only the telegraph message from which to work, began to fill in the holes with his own story. In it he wrote of a three-mile flight that traversed sand dunes and the ocean at a height of sixty feet. Of course, the story was far from correct

The paper in Dayton *assumed* that a flight of under a minute was not newsworthy. The newsmen failed to see how the flight was an important step toward future flights that could change the way people traveled and worked. The newspaper in Norfolk took its assumptions in the opposite direction. It created a story that had the Wright brothers flying their new plane all over the Atlantic Coast. Assumptions caused both papers to miss the true meaning of the flight.

In this case the result of the assumptions was that the newspapers either incorrectly reported the story or did not report on it at all. However, assumptions can cause far greater harm. These situations can test our integrity. They are oftentimes when the incentives we discussed in Chapter Two are headed in opposite directions. Which incentive we follow shapes our character and measures our integrity.

Consider this real-life situation. Back in high school I was at a conference and during a break was visiting with some other students my age. For some reason we began talking about baseball. One person in the group said, "Have you ever noticed there aren't many black catchers in baseball?"

I had never thought about this, and I wondered why this mattered in our discussion.

"Do you think that is because you have to be smart in order to call all of the pitches in the game?" the person said.

Without saying a word, I could tell what everyone else in the group was thinking. Not only was this statement not based on fact, but also it was racist. It was wrong. None of the rest of us believed this statement.

Let's consider the incentives at play here. I may have a social incentive not to speak. I don't know these people very well. If I do take a stand, what might the person who said this think of me? Doing nothing would be much easier and less risky.

However, I also face an important moral incentive. I don't agree with what was just said. Moreover, the statement is racist and wrong. If I say nothing, I allow this statement to be passed off as if it were fact.

I'm ashamed of what I did. Nothing.

We show poor leadership when we make decisions based on assumptions and hearsay. Worse is when we allow blatant lies to go unchallenged.

I would not even have had to say something like, "You're a racist! That isn't right. I don't believe any part of what you just said!"

All I would have had to have said was "What makes you say that?" That simple sentence would suddenly force the person who made the statement to reflect on *why* he or she said it and *why* he or she believed it. That simple question would have helped the other person begin to reflect on his or her previously made assumptions. We must lead with integrity.

Our moral incentive is most often our voice of integrity. Sometimes following the moral incentive may be difficult because it doesn't seem to have the immediate rewards that economic and social incentives can have. That doesn't mean that moral incentives aren't important—they too have much value.

My friend Curtis used to share the example of his baby-blue 1977 Nova. His grandparents had given him the car to drive to college. He would tell you that there was a social incentive for him not to drive this car. The color and style of the vehicle made it seem more fitting for a retiree to drive than a college student.

However, the car was very reliable. It never broke down. It got him to his destination. Curtis always compared that car to a person's integrity. "It's not the outside that matters," he would say. "It's the inside that really counts."

The inside is what counts. The moral incentive is what can be a powerful guide in difficult situations. Remember the gentleman who sat next to me at the church service at Salem? I've often reflected on what that man did. Based on outward appearances, I probably didn't seem to fit in. Because the color of my skin was different, he knew I was most likely a visitor. This man could see that Corey had brought me to church. Why should he bother inviting me to go down front when my friend would be a much more logical choice to do that?

This man had many reasons why he should never have given a single thought to me, but he did give me a thought! He valued me for what was inside me, just as God does. Not only that but also he offered to "walk with me" so that I might feel more at home. His moral incentive told him to reach out to someone else.

How would we have responded if we had been in that man's shoes? We encounter such situations all the time, yet the scene on the outside influences our decisions. Not only should we value the "inside" of others, but also we need to take a good, long look at our own hearts. How have past experiences, perceptions, and assumptions incorrectly influenced our ability to lead? Answering that question will help us lead with a sense of integrity and character that is critical in our journey from the green zone to the summit.

Leadership in the Green Zone

I was in Morristown, New Jersey, to interview the head trainer at the Seeing Eye, the well-known institution that trains dogs that guide the blind. I asked the head trainer what the most difficult part of training these dogs was. I figured that the most difficult part would be helping them learn how to cross a busy city street. Dogs are color-blind, so they can't see the color of stoplights.

When the dog's owner hears traffic moving in a direction parallel to the direction he or she wants to go, he or she will give the command "forward." At that point, the dog must decide whether the street is actually safe to cross. The guide dog may decide to disobey the command based on what it sees, perhaps a car making a right on red. This is called "intelligent disobedience."

The trainer smiled and said, "Intelligent disobedience is difficult, but to me it's not the most challenging part of the training." The dogs usually learn the skill quickly because they too want to avoid being hit by a car.

"So what is the most difficult part of the training?" I asked. He smiled and said, "It's probably that oak tree out there in the front yard."

"Oak tree?" I thought to myself. Why is an oak tree a difficult part of training?

Knowing that I was confused, he said, "How high off of the ground is the lowest limb on that tree?"

"About five feet," I said.

He nodded and replied, "The toughest thing to teach dogs is that once they are leading a blind person on that harness, they can't go underneath that tree anymore. Otherwise we have a lot of people with headaches around here!" He was referring to any overhead obstacle that can be a danger to a person who cannot see yet is not a danger to the dog itself. A tree limb five feet high will not strike a dog, but it will smack a blind person in the face.

Teaching a dog to put itself in the place of the blind person takes time. The dog must realize that it is no longer "just" a dog. It is attached to a human, and the two must function as one. Over time, the dog learns to look at life with a different perspective. The canine's eyes truly must view the world from the human's point of view too.

As leaders, we have to learn to look at life through the eyes of those around us. What is commonplace to us may be new or uncomfortable to others. A Seeing Eye dog learns that it is caring not only for itself but also for the person holding onto its harness. Do we care for others in the same way? The relationship between a Seeing Eye dog and its master depends on the dog looking at life with a new perspective. Learning lessons from the Seeing Eye dog can help us gain a new perspective on life as well. It will help us motivate, recruit, and retain members in the green zone.

CHAPTER 4

The Goal of Goal Setting

NIAGARA FALLS, NY

"In every enterprise consider where you would come out."

—PUBLILIUS SYRUS

Don, a lifelong resident of Niagara Falls, was the "resident historian" of this western New York city thanks to his long tenure at the public library. Now retired from his job, I contacted him to get the scoop on a group of renegades. Don assured me that he had the entire day free to visit with me . . . except for a half hour in the evening when he and his wife had to watch *Jeopardy*. What followed was a intriguing tale over a century in the making.

The story began on October 24, 1901, when a schoolteacher named Ann Edson Taylor came to Niagara Falls. Don relayed that she and her "manager" arrived on a train from her hometown of Bay City, Michigan. She came prepared with her own four and a half foot tall barrel and a small mattress. Those tools were all she needed to attempt a feat that would make news around the world.

It was Ann's forty-sixth birthday and many wondered if it would be her last. (It *was* Ann's birthday, but exactly which birthday may never be known. It seems she often lied about how old she really was. Some say it was actually her 63rd birthday . . . quite a variation). Ann and her crew took the barrel and stuffed the mattress inside. An anvil was placed in the bottom of the barrel to provide ballast. At that point, all that was left was for Ann to get in the barrel and tempt the

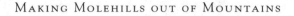

forces of nature. At four o'clock in the evening, the top of the barrel was nailed shut and then lowered into the water above the falls. Soon it hit the brink of the 176-foot rapids and disappeared in the mist below.

Looking back over a century later, what happened that day was probably sheer luck. The fact that the barrel, let alone Ann, survived the plunge is remarkable considering the tremendous power of the falls. Each second, 600,000 gallons of water pours over the falls, thundering thirteen stories into the mist below. When Ann's crew fished out the barrel that day, they pried open the top and Ann emerged groggy but with only a few scratches and a bump on her head. Don added, "I think she already had a bump on her head before she got in the barrel!" Ann Edson Taylor was the first person to go over Niagara Falls in a barrel, beginning a true-to-life legend that lives today.

Ironically, I doubt that many of us had ever heard of Ann Edson Taylor before reading this story. Most of us have heard of people going over the falls in a barrel, but almost no one can tell you the name of anyone who did. Why aren't these individuals remembered? After all, didn't they risk their lives in pursuit of their goals?

So what is the "goal" of goal setting? Is Ann Edson Taylor a good example of someone risking his or her life in pursuit of something no one else had previously been able to attain? Goal setting and achievement are about much more than picking a mark and hitting it; they involve what marks to set, how the marks benefit you, and how reaching the marks affects others.

Why "What I Value" Makes a Difference

On our farm, one of the crops we grow is alfalfa. Depending on the year's rainfall, we may be able to cut and bale a crop of alfalfa four times. The leafy plant grows to a height of about three feet before a bud and then a purple flower blooms.

Alfalfa is an amazing plant, though. It is a perennial. A field of alfalfa may remain productive for five to 10 years. What helps alfalfa survive such growth year after year is its root system. In rich, deep soils, the roots are known to penetrate up to 15 feet deep. The system helps it get the moisture and nutrients it needs to maintain its yearly growth.

The roots are what allow the plant to survive and constant growth to take place. Similarly, if you want to learn to grow as a leader, an important first step is taking a look at your roots. Start by asking "What are the most important 'things' in my life?" Often, people's answers will consist of things such as "family," "friends," "faith," "career," "location," "where I live," and so on.

You may ask, "Why does it matter *what* I value? How does that make any difference when setting and achieving goals?"

For those who know their history, Lakehurst, New Jersey, is synonymous with the Hindenburg airship disaster in 1937. The local historical society even holds its annual picnic at the Lakehurst Naval Air Center, the site of the crash. That's where I traveled to visit with John Ianacone, the last member of the ground crew who is still living today.

The giant airship was one of the most impressive things he had ever seen. "It had two promenade decks in there. They [the German crew] showed us the galley. It was all electric. They even had a piano."

Of course, John's job was not to take tours of the Hindenburg but to help secure it upon landing. The nose of the craft was attached to a mooring mast, but the tail was allowed to move with the wind.

"The tail would sit on this little flat car so that it could go around like a weather vane so that nobody would have to watch it. They would only stay here a few hours; they would come in at six or seven o'clock in the morning and leave at eleven o'clock at night," he explained.

May 6, 1937, was an overcast day. This was to be the first of 18 scheduled round trips from Germany to the United States that year. The ship was carrying 36 passengers and 61 crew members. Strong headwinds delayed the trip, so the Hindenburg could not make its usual morning landing. The approach was delayed until about seven o'clock. The peaceful evening soon turned into a half-minute of sheer terror.

"We could see the whole thing from the nose back to the tail. When it caught on fire, there was a big red glow inside just forward of the tail, and then it broke through the fabric and started to burn. It took 34 seconds from the time the fire started to the time it was completely burned and on the ground. It actually didn't crash; it just settled to the ground."

Despite the fact that the Hindenburg was a falling fireball, John's first reaction was to see what he could do to save lives. "We started to run toward the ship and see if we could help with anybody. We got to the nose before anybody else. As the nose hit the ground, one man walked out. He didn't have a stitch of clothes on him. His shoes, his hair, his skin was all burned off. He died before they got him to an ambulance." It all happened so fast. An airship 800 feet long was gone in half a minute.

Let's think for a moment about the story of the Hindenburg incident. What causes a man like John to run toward the Hindenburg when others were running to safety? What causes a mother to race back inside a burning home to save her baby?

You might be saying, "Well, that's simple. Even though they are heading toward danger, they are trying to save someone's life." That's certainly true. Placed in a similar situation, most people will run toward the danger in order to save someone's life. In other words, "life" is something we highly value. In our earlier discussion of incentives, this would be an example of a moral incentive. We run toward the danger because saving someone's life is the right thing to do.

What else would someone run into a burning house to rescue? My mom used to tell me that she would try to save the family scrapbook because it had so many pictures that she cherished. She found a high value in the memories those pictures held. Each of us has people and items that hold deep value in our lives.

Consider the opening story for this chapter. Is riding inside a barrel and cascading over the brink of Niagara Falls worth risking your life? Not to me. Ann Edson Taylor did it because she thought she would earn fame and fortune if she survived the stunt. However, most people viewed the ride as just what it was: a stunt. Riding over the falls in a barrel didn't do anything to improve the lives of others. It did not hold a strong value in their lives. It was designed only to improve the life of one person, and that person was Ann Edson Taylor herself, if she was lucky enough to survive the ride and get people to pay her for her "accomplishment."

Let's change the situation slightly, though. Let's say Ann Edson Taylor decided to ride over Niagara Falls and half of the proceeds from any money she collected would be given to charity. The public might be more inclined to give because the money would be tied to something some people may value. I might not care whether Ann Edson Taylor received my money, but I might find value in the fact that any money I gave her would now support her charity.

Some roots run deeper than others. My family and faith are deep roots in my life. My work is also a deep root, but it is not as deep as family and faith. The deepness of those roots represents how important each is in our lives.

Take a look at the following diagram of a tree. Earlier in this chapter, we discussed how an alfalfa plant's roots grow deep into the soil to provide it with the nutrients it needs. Similarly, we can use a tree to demonstrate the same thing. The tree represents our lives, and the roots are an example of what we value in our lives. One of the main roots of the tree has been labeled "family" to represent a major thing of value to most people.

We should stop for just a moment to clarify a couple of definitions. Some people might say that "family" is not the real value, but instead we value "love" and our family is just one of the many ways we find "love" or a place to belong. If you prefer to label "love" as the main value and list "family" as one of the ways you find that important quality, that is great. But for our purposes, either will work.

So, if you say "family" is important in your life, what do you do to show that? If my family is supposedly important in my life yet I rarely spend time with my family members or I never call or write, then something is not correct. Either family is not a very deeply rooted value in my life or I'm not spending enough time with my family members to show that to them.

In other words, there should be a relationship between what we value and the amount of time we spend developing that value. Let me give you a real-life example. Before I met my wife, she was very active in many areas of social work, both domestically and internationally. For two years, she lived in Bolivia, the poorest of all South American nations. There she did a variety of things to help the people in rural areas of the country.

When we were dating, we decided to go back to the country on a humanitarian mission. We also took some time to do some sightseeing while we were there. On one of those trips high in the Andes, we were with a tour group of four other people. The place that was provided for us to stay was really just four walls and a roof. This small home was at an altitude of more than 14,000 feet. It had no heat, so you could see your breath even inside the house. Our water bottles froze during the night because it was so cold.

I wasn't feeling well, and Paula was convinced that I was suffering from high-altitude sickness (I thought she was greatly overreacting; I just had a stomach ache, but I couldn't convince her otherwise). One of the ways to combat high-altitude sickness is to drink plenty of fluids. Although I tried to tell Paula I was well hydrated, she insisted that I keep drinking plenty of water.

You can imagine what the consequence was of drinking a gallon of water just before it was time to go to sleep! So, there I was, tucked in a heavy sleeping bag in a room with five other people, one of whom was Paula. About 30 minutes after going to bed, I knew I needed to get out of my sleeping bag and head toward the bathroom (that term was used very loosely; there was a toilet, but it did not have running water. You dipped water from a large barrel and poured it into the toilet in order to make it flush). I tried to get out of the bag quietly, slip on my shoes, and then slowly tiptoe my way out of the room and down the hall to the bathroom.

No sooner did I get on my shoes and start the dark trek to the toilet than I could hear Paula, also getting out of her sleeping bag and following me.

"Are you all right? Are you sick?" she whispered as I felt my way down the hall toward the bathroom.

"I'm fine. It's all that water you made me drink. You can go back to sleep," I whispered, hoping she would be able to go back and get some much-needed rest.

"No, I'm coming with you. I want to make sure you aren't really sick and just lying to me."

At least she didn't follow me all the way into the bathroom but waited just outside the door. The place was so primitive that it had no electricity, so I had to use the minute light on my watch dial to help me find my way. It is amazing how much you can see with that little light when it is pitch-black.

I guess it sounds strange to say that one of the most important points in our dating relationship came in the middle of the night in a Bolivian bathroom. I remember thinking, "How many other people would care about me enough to get out of their sleeping bag in the middle of the night, in freezing temperatures, to follow me to a bath-room without running water, to make sure I was all right?" It wasn't a test, but I knew that Paula really cared about me to do that.

Exactly one year from that night, the two of us were married. The following equation is usually true when it comes to what we value and the amount of time we spend developing those values:

Amount of Time Spent on Value = Deepness of That Value

It takes time for a tree or an alfalfa plant to sink a root deep into the soil. Likewise, it may take time for us to develop relationships with those with whom we work or who serve in our organizations. However, the things we do show that we sincerely value their contributions.

I regularly file stories for a radio network that has about 100 employees. I work there just a few hours a month, but I do know the CEO of the business. He knows that I enjoy writing. One day I dis-covered that he had sent me a book about creative writing with a note that said, "Saw this book and thought it might be a good resource for you." It meant a lot that the CEO of a company for which I worked just a few hours a month would take time to do that for me. He was developing the roots of this company by taking time to show his sincere appreciation for the work of his employees.

What can you do to show the value you place in others? I was vis-iting with my dad, and I asked him, "From all of your experience, what do you think is the most important thing you can do to moti-vate employees?"

He had a quick and simple answer: "Set them up to succeed."

I asked him what he meant by that statement. He explained: "A lot of times, when people come to work in a new job, it is kind of over-whelming in the beginning. You have to be careful about telling them what they need to do. You forget that you have been around these jobs for several years and they are just beginning. So I always try to start them out with small jobs that I think they will have a high probability of doing correctly. Everybody likes to do something right, so that gives them confidence when I ask them to do something bigger."

He continued to explain that his goal was for employees to have a series of small successes every day they came to work. Even when they may fail at something, they aren't demoralized. They have some past successes that will give them confidence to keep going.

Making Time for Leadership

For one of my radio broadcasts, I interviewed two forestry researchers who were developing climate models based on tree rings. They would go to stream beds and look for old logs that had been covered by mud. Specifically, they were hoping to find pieces of tree trunks that were 1,000 to 2,000 years old that had been preserved by mud when the stream channel had shifted.

They then counted the tree rings and measured the distances between each, using the tree rings to put together a 1,000-year time line of the climate of the earth. It is interesting research, and it tells us a lot about weather patterns over centuries.

A tree ring is a measure of growth. In our example, the tree rings also help measure our growth. Think about it: if a tree has a poor growing season, it can't go back and expand previous rings when a great growing season comes along years later. Once that year has passed, nothing can be done to affect leadership growth.

It is the same with our personal growth. Once time is gone, we can't recapture it. It stands to reason that we develop a plan to better use our time.

The idea is to find areas of our lives where we could use our time more wisely. People are often tempted to say, "I don't have any extra time; there is no way I can fit anything else in."

We often believe we don't have time to do something, but what we are really saying is that we don't *value* the task enough to make time for it. If something is important enough to us, we will make time for it.

If I needed to go to a doctor's office every day to receive a vaccination in order to live and not die, I would find the time to get that shot every day. The issue is not about making time; it is about weighing the importance of the item. That's the reason many of us have difficulty with time management. It is not that we don't have enough time; it is that we have difficulty prioritizing our time.

Instead of always looking at a "to do" list, perhaps you need a "don't do" list. This is why it is important that you begin by looking at what you value in life and what you will do to develop these values.

By recognizing what will help us and others grow, we will prioritize our time accordingly. This is not always an easy task. Unexpected emergencies sometimes derail our schedule. But the idea is to change our *habits* and in turn change our lives for the better.

You might keep a precise log of what you do during a day. Write down the times when you spend even a couple of minutes making a phone call. What you will find is that little pieces of time add up to large chucks of time that you might use more wisely. Perhaps you could rearrange your schedule to better accomplish all that you need to do.

Working Smarter, Not Harder

Leadership is hard work, but using the above principles will help you work smarter and make the most of your time. Let me give you a real-life example of how leadership strategies can help you make the most of your abilities.

When I was in college, I always looked forward to one special week of college—finals week. I'm not trying to be funny! Finals week was really my favorite time of the semester because it was the easiest week of the year. Why? I was a student who applied a system to learning. Keep in mind that I was not valedictorian or salutatorian of my class.

During college I took a difficult chemistry course to complete my science requirements for my degree. This was a large class of more than 500 students at the University of Missouri. Although this was a very large group, twice each week, we were assigned to a lab group of 20 students. Our teaching assistant wanted to help us get the best grade we could in the class. In order to keep tables on where we stood, every two weeks he handed us a slip of paper with our class rank and our average grade in the class.

I knew this would be a very tough class, so I studied very hard, and that hard work paid off. Six weeks into the class, I was handed a slip of paper that said I ranked first in the class! I was certainly not the smartest person in the class. There were pre-med majors and many others students working toward science degrees who were in that class and I knew they had more smarts in the science field than I did.

I finished in the top 10 of that chemistry class of 500 students. Why was a person who wasn't as "smart" in that position? It all relates to how the majority of students will study. If a typical college course has five equally weighted tests during the year and we polled the students at the conclusion of the course as to how much time they spent studying for each of those tests, the majority would say they spent more time studying for the last test. Why? Because their final grade depended heavily on what they received for a grade on that last test.

In reality, each test was weighted the same, yet they had not invested the time earlier in the course to study for the tests, so they lagged behind where they had hoped to be. Their initial slow start was still holding them back at the end of the course.

Conversely, I can count on one hand the number of times I need to get an A on the final test to keep an A for the class. I remember that for one class, I needed a 23% on the final to keep my A in the class! I received better grades in college than I did in high school. I believe that most of that was due to the way I approached my class-work. I always tried to invest more time studying hard early in the semester because I knew it would pay big dividends toward the end of the course.

That plan won't work perfectly every time, but it will work a bulk of the time. It's all a part of working smarter, not harder. It's a way to use your time to its maximum. Great leaders look for those little advantages that create big results.

In this chapter we've moved from the green zone to the yellow zone. The yellow zone in the leadership model represents our growth. Understanding our values and goals prepares us for growth. Using good time-management skills also helps us accomplish more and pushes us through the yellow zone more quickly. The yellow zone is about the skills we need to expand our abilities and grow in all facets of our daily lives.

Within the yellow zone we use the tree as our model. It reminds us that what we value gives us strength for life ahead. It also helps us to see the goals we have for several parts of our life. Finally, the trunk reminds us that we have a finite amount of time, so making the most of each day is critical in helping our "tree" grow.

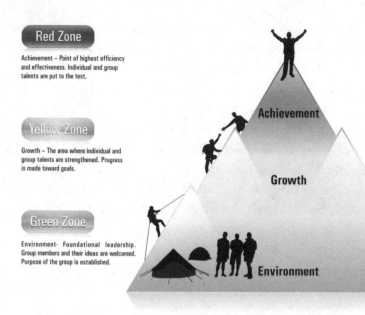

Red Zone

Achievement – Point of highest efficiency and effectiveness. Individual and group talents are put to the test.

Yellow Zone

Growth – The area where individual and group talents are strengthened. Progress is made toward goals.

Green Zone

Environment- Foundational leadership. Group members and their ideas are welcomed. Purpose of the group is established.

Just as roots tend to branch underneath the surface, the tree's limbs branch above the trunk. The branching of a tree is an important concept in personal goal setting. Too many times, goal setting is simply setting a high mark and then doing everything you can to hit it. If you don't hit the mark, you feel that you failed and that all the time spent on the task was worthless. The branching nature of goals tells us something far different.

When I was a junior in college, I ran for a national office in a national student leadership organization. Over the course of eight months, I spent several hours each week preparing for the interviews that took place at the national convention. Forty candidates vied for six positions, and we all had to go through six rounds of interviews plus take a written test.

If I was selected to be one of the six national officers, I would leave college for one year and work for the organization. If I wasn't selected, I would go back to school the next day and resume my class-work. I remember thinking that if I didn't get an office, "All of this will have been a waste. I will have spent a good chunk of my life run-ning after a goal that I didn't achieve."

Whenever we begin to think this way, we lose sight of the "branching" nature of goals. At that point in my life, "national office" was a goal on one branch of a much larger tree. Because I focused so much on that goal, I began to view it not as a branch but as the entire tree.

Don't get me wrong; I wanted to be selected to a national office. I want you to work hard and achieve the goals you have in your life. However, remember to keep two important things in mind. First, each goal we set is part of a much bigger picture. Don't feel that a failure to reach a specific goal dooms the entire tree. Second, realize that the pursuit of a goal strengthens our abilities to reach future goals.

Notice what a small portion of the overall tree one goal is. The pursuit of our goals helps us grow. That's why failures are rarely fail-ures. Even when we miss our ultimate mark, the growth we achieve is helping us to expand our abilities. At the time of my pursuit of the national office goal, I thought that I would have wasted a lot of valu-able time if I didn't get elected. Now I realize that I was learning public speaking and interviewing skills that continue to help me in a variety of areas today.

Also keep in mind that rarely will one event in life totally change what we decide to make our life's work. Today I see that whether or not I accomplished my goal of getting a national office, I would have been doing exactly what I'm doing today. Certainly some small things might have changed, but, overall, this one goal did not change my entire life. Keeping this in mind helps us to live with a better per-spective of how "successes" and "failures" really affect what we do.

Henry Ford spoke of how even the little failures of life move us toward higher branches on our tree. He said, "Life is a series of experiences, each one of which makes us bigger, even though it is hard to realize this. For the world was built to develop character, and we must learn that the setbacks and grieves which we endure help us in our marching onward."

Growing a Balanced Leader

I think everyone probably knows the cliché that says, "Don't put all of your eggs in one basket." In other words, diversify your abilities. Consider the mental, physical, social, and spiritual aspects of your life. Each area can have an affect on the others. If I set all of my goals in the mental area of my life and don't do anything to develop my social skills or develop a network of friends, then I might become a very smart and very lonely person.

While we need to soar with our strengths, we must be sure not to let other areas of our lives hold us back from being well-rounded leaders. We might not be perfectly balanced, but we do need to work to develop all areas of our lives. Otherwise, a weak area can actually slow the progress of goals in other areas. The branches of a tree usually grow on all sides of the trunk. If not, the tree will become lopsided and fall over. The same is true for our lives if we don't grow in a balanced way.

We've used most of this chapter to talk about how a tree represents our lives. The one thing we haven't talked about is where the tree is planted.

I was once interviewing a young man who owned an orange grove near Vero Beach, Florida. I was really interested in the process of growing the fruit and getting the produce to market. I asked whether he used a machine to shake the tree and collect the ripe fruit, a mechanical substitute for hand picking.

"No, we don't use one of the machines here," he replied.

I was a little surprised that he didn't use one because his grove was a large operation and I was sure he had the means to purchase one.

I asked the logical follow-up, "Why don't you have one?"

"The soil here around Vero Beach is very sandy," he explained. "The soil isn't dense enough to firmly hold the roots of the orange trees. If we use a machine to shake the trees, it dislodges the roots and causes many of them to die."

In other words, the soil could not support such a root shaking by the mechanical picker. How extensive of a root system these trees had mattered very little because the soil would not support the shaking.

The same is true for the life of a leader. It doesn't matter how deep your roots are if you are planted in the wrong location. Surround yourself with people who will challenge you to become the best person you can be. Place yourself in situations that help you take small steps forward. In other words, find soil that facilitates growth.

Benchmarking

A few years ago I decided that I needed to become more physically fit, so I began jogging. Because I lived on the farm, I had plenty of country roads on which I could run and see the countryside while getting in a workout.

After several months of running, I was challenged by one of my best friends, also a runner, to enter a 10K race with him. Troy is a good athlete. He was all-conference in basketball and still holds the high-jump record at our school. I, on the other hand, am just a mediocre athlete. But, I thought it would be good for me to train to run the 6.2 miles (10K) and see how well I could do.

I should have known that I was in trouble when one mile into the race a woman in the over-60 age division passed me. I never passed her back. Halfway through the race, Troy, who was well ahead of me, stopped and let me catch up. We ran the rest of the race together. He could have taken off from me at any point, but I appreciated that he wanted to run with me and help me push my own pace.

I finished the race in just over 52 minutes. The winner of the race crossed the finish line 20 minutes ahead of me. Would it be realistic for me to cut 20 minutes off of my time the next time I race? Probably not. I would die in the process. Could I shave 30 seconds off of my time? With continued training, I probably could.

I did not realize that a picture would be taken of Troy and me crossing the finish line. As you can see, this race was more difficult for one of us. While Troy appears to be somewhere in the green zone, I am definitely in the red zone. In fact, I am bordering on reaching beyond the red zone to the black zone—death.

When I ran my 10K race, Troy stopped to run with me. He didn't stop because he was tired. He stopped in order to help push me to improve my own time. We each need friends like that, people who will urge us to be the best we can be.

Every time I run, I set my own personal goal for that day. It is my personal benchmark that I'm trying to reach. If I'm going to be running in a race, I will set a series of benchmarks each day and will steadily attempt to lower my time as the race draws nearer.

Just because the race is more difficult for some, doesn't mean it is not worth running.

Benchmarks are simply smaller goals that help us reach our larger goals in life. Setting and achieving little goals each day helps us keep positive momentum in reaching the bigger things in life.

Don't get caught up in running races against others. The most important race you will run is the race against yourself. If you set the goal to improve your best each day, you will eventually begin to better your best every day. Set benchmarks that help you keep achieving small steps in a positive direction. What is a green zone activity for some will be a red zone activity for others. Don't let that discourage you from setting and achieving your goals.

However, just because I can work at improving my running ability doesn't mean that I need to make track and field my career. I don't want to be too negative, but I doubt I will ever be able to run a 10K race in 32 minutes. I can certainly work to run faster than 52 minutes, but shaving 20 minutes from my time is going to be extremely difficult.

But that's all right, because my career is not directly dependent on how fast I run a 10K. So why do I run, then? I run and do other physical activities because I know that I need to stay in shape. If I am not physically fit, then other parts of my life will suffer.

Our careers should be based on our strengths and things we enjoy doing. That doesn't mean that every part of our jobs will be fun. Remember that I have to scoop manure in my job, but, overall, I really enjoy working on our farm and ranch.

We began this chapter speaking about Ann Edson Taylor and others who have attempted to go over Niagara Falls in a barrel. Are they good examples of what yellow zone leadership is? Not really.

We pay tribute to those who risk their lives, or even lose their lives, in pursuit of a "purposeful" goal. Not all heroes have giant memorials built in their honor, but we usually honor and remember people for what they do for others. We pay tribute to how they helped society or bettered the lives of those around them.

Just because we have moved to the yellow zone does not mean that we should lose sight of the foundation that was laid in the green zone. It is in the green zone that we establish the purpose for what we do. If we suddenly lose sight of the purpose when we get to the yellow zone, our lives become all about *us* achieving goals that affect only *us*.

The daredevils who survived their ride over Niagara Falls in a barrel took such a risk for their *own* glory. (In fact, Ann Edson Taylor "passed the hat" after her success in order to reap a monetary gain, though Don said she never became wealthy or a household name.) True leaders believe in causes that reach far beyond their own welfare. They work to improve the lives of others and to build communities. That's what it means to live life in the yellow zone.

CHAPTER 5
Efficiency and Effectiveness
JEFFERSON CITY, MO

"A sensible man never embarks on an enterprise until he can see his way clear to the end of it."

— AESOP

I t was my first day as a talk show host. Since I am in the radio business, I had been around talk shows for many years and I thought I knew quite a bit about how such shows worked. Still, I was nervous about my first solo appearance as a guest host. Could I ask intelligent questions of my guests? Could I handle the callers? I was excited and apprehensive all at the same time.

I had lined up a great guest for my inaugural show. He was a young entrepreneur who had created a space tourism business and he planned to offer trips into outer space within a few years. In fact, 150 people had already paid several hundred dollars to "hold" their place in line, to get one of the first tickets into outer space.

I read over notes about the business. I read magazine articles about the space tourism industry. I knew the topic would generate plenty of interest from many listeners, and I was ready to discuss the subject with plenty of knowledge to spare.

It was four minutes past the top of the hour. Two more minutes and the theme music would begin to play. At that moment, the producer, sitting just across the glass from me, gave me an important message via my headset. No one at the space tourism business knew where the president was. He had disappeared. Until they could locate him, I was on my own.

So there I was. I had the perfect topic, but no guest. I don't really know what I said during the first ten-minute segment of the show. I recited every fact I knew about the solar system. I muttered useless facts about planets like Neptune and Pluto. I read from the press releases and magazine articles I had researched. All the while, the producer stayed on the line as an entire company searched for their president.

The good news was I had filled the first ten minutes. The bad news was, I had used up every piece of material I had and I still had another forty-four minutes to fill!

When they finally found the absent-minded president, he was kind enough to come on the air and fill six whole minutes before he jetted off to another meeting. That was it. The interview I had set up weeks ahead of time, the interview that was to last an entire hour, lasted six minutes.

Now was the time when I would see if I had what it took to be a talk show host. I asked my audience questions. Were any of them still listening? Would any of them call in to save me? I rambled on, looking at my computer screen, hoping the blinking cursor would soon change to a caller's name.

Almost all talk shows use a call screener. The host is then able to look at a computer screen and see the caller's name, city, or state, and the topic they wish to discuss. I could handle up to five calls at one time. At this moment, I would settle for just one.

Finally, I could see the producer frantically typing me a message. There it was. "Billy" from Missouri was on the line. I didn't wait long enough to see what he wished to discuss. I was already stating that we were headed to line number four (as if line numbers one through three were already filled) to talk to Billy in Missouri.

Billy sounded as if he had just come out of hibernation. His slow drawl and crude English didn't make him the most articulate caller I could have received.

He said, "Ya know where I'd like ta go if I was gonna take a trip in ta outa space?"

Did I really want to know? Did anybody want to know? Billy was all I had. I was still staring at approximately thirty-four minutes to fill. So I gladly said, "Where do you want to go, Billy?"

Billy said, "If I got ta go anywhere I could want ta go in the una verse, I'd think I'd go to Utopia. Ya know where Utopia is?"

Utopia. I had always been told that Utopia was a fictional place, an imaginary state of well being. There was no exact place called "Utopia." It was wherever a person wanted it to be.

At this point I began to concentrate on the red "kill" button next to my monitor. What was "utopia" to Billy? Could his definition really go out over the airwaves? The way Billy sounded, I thought he was already in a state of Utopia. In fact, he might be smoking something right now that was sending him to Utopia.

I inched my hand closer to the button that would drop Billy from the airwaves (the talk show operated on a delay. Anything Billy said was delayed three seconds before it went out over the air).

Billy demanded, "Do ya know where Utopia is?"

I stammered, "I don't think I know."

Suddenly it seemed that Billy came out of his slow drawl. Intelligence suddenly seemed to enter his brain and shed light on his words. The southern Missouri hillbilly was about to change into a great man of science.

"Utopia is one of Jupiter's moons." (That's not exactly true. "Europa" is one of Jupiter's moons. But it sounded close enough to me and I doubt many of the listeners knew much about the moons of Jupiter).

Billy continued. "I would go there because of its many unique features." We were now on a roll as Billy began to describe the many features as if he were Carl Sagan's long-lost brother.

I wasn't about to let Billy go. He was the only thing saving the program. It turned out Billy was a former aerospace engineer (if he wasn't, he certainly put on a good show that saved me for several minutes). I continued to ask him questions as if he were my intended guest.

I learned early on the vital importance of having a back-up plan. I did not carry any resources into the studio that day, save the notes for my intended topic. Today, I always bring several newspapers with me and have a few magazine articles on hand if I am interviewed or if I must host a show. I can always begin to discuss an interesting topic and generate some discussion on the airwaves.

Planning effective meetings, conferences, and conventions is a lot like running a talk show. You've got to line up guests and know your topic. You have to make the information relevant and interesting to the group. You must engage the group in the topic so that each group member wants to be a part of the program. Time is of the essence because you have to finish at a specific time and make room for commercials too.

I have seen plenty of disastrous meetings over the years. Most of the mishaps, like my first stint as a talk show host, could have been avoided. The consequences of each tell us a lot about the importance leaders have in facilitating a meeting, a convention, or any other type of gathering. Unfortunately, this topic is often an afterthought. Like my shaky beginning as a talk show host, let me describe just how bad things can go if you don't plan ahead when running a meeting.

I was once at a large convention with about 5,000 people in attendance. The convention involved a variety of speakers and award recognitions. On this night of the convention, one of the organization's most prestigious awards was to be presented. The award had lots of applicants who were then pared down to four finalists.

Now with the finalists on stage, the emcee said, "And your winner is . . . Amber Worthington from Santa Fe!" The crowd erupted with applause. Amber's family was so excited to see her win. Imagine the disappointment when someone appeared from backstage and whispered to the emcee, who returned to the podium to announce, "I'm afraid I made a mistake." A mistake! How can you make a mistake when you are reading the winner of the most important award of the evening?

I've seen speakers fall off of a stage. I've seen award recipients wander haplessly before the audience, not knowing where they were supposed to go.

At one event where I was speaking, the emcee struggled to make it through a short, typed introduction, an introduction he could have practiced because he had it for several weeks. The disjointed intro hit the climax when I was introduced as "Andrea McCrea." Not only was my name wrong but also I had switched from male to female.

On another occasion, an emcee became flustered when she could not find her script on the podium before her. After scrambling through countless papers, she finally slammed her three-ring binder shut and walked off stage, leaving the award recipients stranded, awaiting the announcement of the winner.

What may be the most disastrous events, though, are things that happen at smaller meetings or in the workplace that go largely unseen. They are the little things that can cause a group or business to wither into a small group of individuals with no direction.

Keeping our mountain model in mind, we need to have a plan for organizing our assault on the summit. As Everest climber Alan Hobson noted, preparing for the journey takes three to seven years. Much of that time is spent in meetings, raising monetary support for the expedition, and preparing all of the individual pieces that go into the feat.

How You Can Create Your Own Meeting Disaster

Let me tell you exactly what to do if you want to make a mess of a meeting, whether at work, for an organization, or even at a large convention. Here are some of the biggest mistakes we make:

1. We don't have an agenda, or, if we do have an agenda, it contains too many items or irrelevant items.
2. We don't have regard for time. The meeting drags and people are upset because they've "wasted" time at the meeting.
3. The group members feel there is nothing in this meeting for them. They are disconnected from the purpose of the group.
4. Members don't get a chance to express their ideas.
5. Those in charge of the meeting are not prepared.

This is a very brief list; however, it covers some of the biggest items that go wrong. Some things will depend on the size of the meeting. It may be a small group of 10 or a large convention session of 1,000, but in general, these same points apply.

When I'm in charge of planning a meeting, my goal is to always adjourn the session ahead of time. In most people's minds, nothing makes for a great meeting like getting out ahead of time! There is a huge psychological difference in ending a meeting five minutes early versus five minutes late. It's only five minutes one way or the other, but in most of our minds, it's either "early" or "late."

So, how do you control the clock? Believe it or not, you *do* have a lot of control over how long a meeting may last. In smaller groups, I may tell the members exactly when we plan to adjourn. For larger convention sessions, this may be printed in a program. If you think you have about 70 minutes of items to cover, don't set a time line to be done in one hour. Give yourself an hour and a half and end early!

This should not be an excuse for just extending your time line to fit your agenda. You need to look at the agenda ahead of time and do all you can to trim it to only the relevant items for this meeting. Perhaps some items would be best handled by a smaller committee that could then report to the larger group.

I've been a part of some groups that use parliamentary procedure to limit the time for debate on certain items. This can be an effective tool to control meeting time. If you are not familiar with Robert's Rules of Order, you should take time to understand the basics. It is very important for the leaders of meetings to know how to effectively lead a business meeting, so take time to understand parliamentary procedure. Make sure your planning committee or officer team meets ahead of time to go over the agenda. This will help you keep the meeting moving.

What about speakers who take too much time? Sometimes there is little you can do once a speaker takes the microphone. You need to emphasize to that speaker exactly how much time he or she has on your program. You may want to allow a little extra time in your agenda in case this speaker runs long.

If it is a smaller meeting, you may work out a signal with speakers ahead of time so that they know when their time is almost up. If you discuss this ahead of time, it might be perfectly appropriate for you to stand in the back of the room and hold up one hand when they have five minutes remaining. Again, work this out ahead of time and don't do anything that would distract from the presentation or annoy the audience. The best signals are so subtle that no one will ever know that you've in fact signaled the speaker.

The Perfect Idea

The answers to our organization's most difficult problems are most often sitting within the room. However, several obstacles can prevent people from sharing. Here are a couple of techniques you can use to better facilitate this portion of a meeting.

Anonymous Sharing—In some groups, individuals may be reluctant to share their thoughts. This might be the case for a number of reasons. Perhaps they are simply shy. They may believe that if they share their ideas, others in the group will think they are stupid and it will reflect poorly on them. Or, they don't think they have great ideas and therefore won't share them because they aren't as good as other people's ideas.

One way to help overcome this barrier is to give each person in your group several sticky notes. On each note people can write down their idea(s). Only one idea should be placed on each note. The notes are then collected and posted on a wall where everyone can see them. Similar ideas are grouped together. In this way, the wall is transformed into clusters of notes. This allows for a visual representation of what the group is thinking.

Don't simply go with the cluster that appears largest. You might find one lone note with an idea completely different from any other ideas on the wall. Read the groupings of ideas and get feedback from the group. This method allows everyone to share his or her ideas anonymously and provides the group with plenty of material with which to work.

Small Group Sharing—Smaller groups are often a better way for individuals to have their voices heard. By breaking into smaller groups, individuals have face-to-face contact. A scribe can record all the ideas that are shared. The small group may even vote on the top two or three ideas and then share them with the group.

This method avoids the time of writing ideas on paper and then grouping them in clusters on a wall. It still allows people to feel fairly comfortable with sharing their ideas within the confines of a small group.

Serving as Emcee

The emcee is a very important part of your event. Some conferences will have only one emcee while others may use a rotation of people who will come to the podium to introduce speakers, give awards, and recognize special guests. Regardless of how this role is divided, the following tips will help you conduct the event appropriately.

1. Practice! If there is one thing that groups need to do in order to run a more effective meeting, it is to simply practice. If you will be introducing someone, practice reading the part aloud several times.

Practice saying your parts with the actual microphone. Have people tell you whether you are speaking at a volume that can be heard in the back of the room. Practice a system for handing out awards. Read through the list of award recipients and try to get the correct pronunciation of their names.

What I'm saying sounds very simple, yet most people will never invest the time to practice the role of emcee. Practicing your role as an emcee is vital to your success.

2. Remember that you are not the entertainment. Professional speaker and emcee Brian Lee once said that good emcees remember that they are the frame around the picture. Just as a frame holds a picture in place so that others can see, an emcee helps tie the meeting together and display the talents and recognition to be bestowed on those on the program.

You do not need to be a comedian to be an emcee! If you are worried about what you will say, it is fine to have a script. Don't worry about trying to be funny or cute, and never, ever try to do something that would make others feel uncomfortable or bad about themselves. I've seen emcees try to embarrass the speaker. Others feel that jokes are necessary. All of these examples are attempts to make you the picture instead of the frame. Remember that your job is to showcase others and keep the meeting running effectively.

Given a choice between funny and timely, almost every audience will choose timely. If you have the ability to do both, that is excellent. However, don't try to be funny. Just keep the agenda on time and on task and the audience will value the job you have done.

3. You help keep the event focused and timely. No one likes a meeting that drags on too long and goes over its allotted time. While you can't control every single part of the program, you can do a lot to influence its outcome.

Communicate how much time each part of the program should take. If you have speakers on the program, make sure to clearly tell them how much time they have. They may want you to signal them at a certain time in their presentation. As mentioned earlier, work this out ahead of time.

4. Award Recognition—or Lack Thereof. If there is any place in a program that will drag and cause the meeting to run long, it is usually the awards program. I've helped organize ceremonies where literally hundreds of people have received awards during a one-hour session. Here are some important tips to give people the recognition they deserve and make your program run on time.

Practice a system for handing out awards. For larger programs, I will have organization officers walk though the way they will hand out plaques and move people on and off the stage. Doing this ahead of time is critical.

The great convention invention: the power clap. The power clap is to a meeting what the wave is to sports fans. It's a way to build enthusiasm and recognition, and it saves time. That's why I call it the "great convention invention." A power clap is simply one clap from the entire audience. You will need to explain to the audience ahead of time that you will count down, "three, two, one," and then they will all clap one time at the exact same time.

Once you've explained the power clap, you need to set up your awards recognition something like this: "We have many great sponsors who've helped to make this session possible tonight. We want not only to recognize them but also to show them how much we appreciate their help. After I read each company's or organization's name, please generate a large power clap for each!" At this point, you will begin to read through the list of names. The crowd will simply give a power clap after each.

I've noticed that the age of the audience doesn't matter; everyone seems to love the power clap. It adds a little excitement to the meeting. It's quick and keeps people involved. You can still give a big round of applause after the entire list is complete. There is a huge difference between saying "I will read the list of sponsors; please hold all applause until I have finished reading the list" and saying "Please join me in giving one big power clap after I read the names of each of our sponsors." Both take the same time. The audience is simply providing a power clap where you are already taking a half-second pause between reading each name.

One warning for using the power clap: only use it for long lists of names when those mentioned will not be coming forward to receive plaques. When single individuals or small groups are being honored and brought forward to receive an award, they should receive more than a simple clap.

Practice names ahead of time. If you are handing out awards, look at the list of names ahead of time. If you don't recognize a name, try to find someone who can help you with the correct pronunciation. If you still don't know the correct way to say a name, pick a way to say it and stick to it. Please, please, please do not stumble three or four times over the name and then say, "I'm sorry about that." If you say it once and say it with confidence, the only people in the crowd who will know that you didn't say it correctly will be the people who know the person. If you stumble over it, everyone will know that you didn't know what you were doing.

When disaster strikes. Sometimes it happens: a plaque or certificate might get out of order or someone might receive the wrong item. All you need to do is simply tell the recipient that you will help to make the switch off the stage. Don't spend time on stage trying to fix an award problem. Most problems can be solved to the side of the audience, which will allow the program to continue. In the case of a major problem, just stop and find your place. This is better than plowing ahead and generating more mistakes.

What's the big deal? You may not think that practicing award ceremonies is a big deal, but it can make or break the timing of your meeting. Think about it. Even if you had only 50 award recipients and

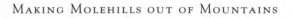

you saved just 15 seconds on each, you would gain 12 and a half minutes. Little amounts of time add up. I've had programs in which more than 750 people have been recognized. If you saved just two and a half seconds per name, you will have gained over a half hour of time.

Don't make the award recognition look hurried, but do look for little ways you can make the program look sharp and give people the congratulations they deserve.

5. Introducing Speakers and Guests

One important part of the role of emcee is introducing guests and speakers. Sometimes guest speakers will have an introduction already written. Ask them whether they would like you to read it as written. Some speakers will have a full-page introduction and expect you to read every word of it.

However, many times speakers will give you a biography for you to write their introduction or they may not have any kind of introduction. In these cases, you will need to either edit the material you've been given or write something from scratch.

Here are three important points to keep in mind when writing the introduction:

Why is the speaker on the program? If this is one of the main speakers on your program, begin with a sentence that shows the person's relevance to the agenda and the organization. Some people in your audience may wonder why the speaker has been invited to address the group. One sentence that addresses the purpose of the speaker helps answer this question.

How does the speaker fulfill that purpose? Once you've established the purpose the speaker fills on the agenda, provide the speaker's credentials that support this. If you are editing or writing an introduction for a speaker, look for three or four main points to include.

If the speaker has a long list of accomplishments, you may want to include a couple of extra points, but in general, an introduction

Our theme for this year's banquet is "Discover the Power." We want each member of our school and our community to discover the power they have to make a positive impact on the world around them. This way we can reach our fullest capabilities individually and inspire our fellow members to do the same. Our speaker tonight knows much about helping people discover their leaderhsip powers. He served as state president of our organization in 1991–92 and as a national officer in 1993–94. In 1995 he joined "Unlimited Skies" one of Chicago's inter city outreach teams counseling "at risk" youth. He also speaks to hundreds of civic organizations each year stressing the importance of reaching personal success. Would you please welcome from Richmond, Indiana, a past organization officer, counselor and leadership speaker, Mr. Doug Belmont.

WHY ←

HOW ←

PLACE, TITLE, NAME! ←

that provides three or four key credentials will give the audience a good idea of the speaker's background.

The last sentence: FROM, TITLE, NAME. If you remember one thing about writing strong introductions, remember how to write the last sentence of an introduction. The last sentence should tell the audience where the speaker is from, his or her title, and his or her name. The name should be the last two words in an introduction. All other sentences should be building toward this name.

For example, the last sentence might be delivered as "Please welcome, from Detroit, Michigan, the founder and president of Unlimited Skies, Mr. Doug Belmont." Don't give an introduction in which the first words out of your mouth are "Doug Belmont is our speaker tonight." This is the equivalent of a big-time basketball announcer saying, "Andrew McCrea, he's a junior standing six foot two, playing guard, and his number is 23." No, no, no. A better introduction would be "Starting at guard, a six-foot-two-inch junior, number 23, ANDREW MCCREA!!"

You don't have to sound like a basketball arena announcer when you deliver the introduction, but you should have enthusiasm, and you should build excitement toward delivering the speaker's name.

I've included a sample introduction written in the above format. Notice that an arrow labeled "Why" points to the beginning of the introduction. This denotes the sentence that answers why this speaker is on the program. A second arrow labeled "How" points to the body of the introduction. These sentences are the biography of the speaker; these credentials should answer how the speaker will fulfill the purpose of the meeting or program.

The bottom arrow points to the very important last sentence. Remember to structure the words to provide where the speaker is from, his or her title, and his or her name. This is the most important sentence in the introduction and should be delivered slightly louder than the rest of the introduction. This adds energy to your words.

On the basis of the specific event, the length of the introduction will change, but the overall format should not. If this is a meeting of only 10 people and the speaker is known to the audience, then you will probably not need to add quite as much information as you would in front of an audience of 1,000 people who have never met the speaker.

You can judge the situation and adjust accordingly. However, don't use the fact that you are in front of a small gathering as an excuse to deliver an poor introduction. You can be casual yet confident, and this sets the tone for the speaker who is about to present his or her information.

Self-Introductions. Sometimes you will be called upon to introduce yourself. **The format for a self-introduction is the exact opposite of**

the introduction of a speaker. You now begin with your name, title, and where you are from. You then provide the audience with three or four facts about yourself. After this, you may include a few sentences about why you are a part of the group and/or your future plans.

Just as a speaker's introduction lists credentials that show how the person fits the purpose of the group, the items you share in the self-introduction should be examples of what you do that builds on the mission of the group you represent. If you are delivering a self-introduction and are not representing a specific group, then this portion of your self-introduction simply lists things you do that demonstrate your purpose in life.

If appropriate, you can use the last sentence of your self-introduction to answer the question "Why?" Why are you devoting time to the activities you just mentioned? Perhaps the items you mentioned are preparing you for a future career, or maybe they show how they have helped prepare you for the career you now have.

Self-introductions shouldn't be long or mechanical. However, you can use this format to deliver a focused, one-minute autobiography of yourself. The self-introduction can be lengthened or shortened depending on the situation. In casual conversation, you are already delivering a 15-second version of the self-introduction.

For example, if I meet someone for the first time, I might say, "Hello, I'm Andrew McCrea, the communication director for XYZ in King City, Missouri." I just delivered the first sentence of a self-introduction. If the conversation continues, I'm probably answering the "How?" and "Why?" questions in the information I'm providing.

Some of you are saying, "Wow, we've spent a lot of time on things that are really simple." Perhaps speaker introductions and self-introductions are commonplace, yet I see them poorly delivered on many occasions. Think about how you can use these times to clearly communicate with your audience.

Advice on Advisors

If you are a high school or college student, you are likely involved in a group that has an advisor/a teacher/a professor who may volunteer to be the adult sponsor. I don't know how many times I've heard someone say, "Our group can't accomplish anything because we don't have a good advisor." I'm not going to say that this statement is never correct, but I often hear those same advisors say, "We'd have a great organization if my students were more motivated to participate."

So what's the problem? The same principles we discussed in the chapter on motivation apply here, but I'd like to tell you about some other things you can do to help the situation. The number one thing that I have seen propel these groups to success is each side making an investment in the other's work.

Realize that an advisor may have to perform the role of group sponsor for little or no compensation. The advisor may have been told that he or she had to be responsible for your group. If the members of your group believe in the mission of the local chapter, maybe each of you could take turns volunteering one hour a week or a month to help the advisor. You could say to the advisor, "We know that you have lots of things going on in your life, but we've agreed that we can volunteer one hour each Monday, Wednesday, and Friday to help you. Maybe you need a letter or an e-mail sent to our members, or perhaps you need help making calls to find judges for one of our competitions. Whatever it is, you can be guaranteed that you will have one or more of our members here three days a week to help you."

If you and your membership make a statement like that to an advisor, almost every single advisor out there will suddenly become more motivated to help you. You are helping your advisor help you! If you had just six people agree to do this, you would have to volunteer only one hour every other week. That's a pretty small investment if you believe in the purpose of the group.

Advisors, if you can agree to help students in competitions or projects, that is a great way to invest in what is important to them. I once had an advisor who believed in me and wanted to help me improve my public speaking. When I entered a competition, this advisor took it upon himself to find other teachers who would be willing to listen to my speech and give me feedback. It probably took him 10 minutes to set this up. It meant a lot to me because he wanted to invest in my future.

Invest in each other and you will often find that your organization will suddenly gain motivation from its members and advisors to accomplish much. Also, realize that while an advisor may stay in the position for several years, the student leaders may continue to rotate through the group. This means that new officers are at a disadvantage because they do not have experience.

I was recently working with some organization officers who had a great idea of how to build great officer teams. They realized that because a high percentage of their group's officers graduated each year, the new officers were left with few experienced leaders that could help guide the next group. The group seemed to struggle with many of the same problems each year.

In order to overcome this, each officer took time to create a small notebook. The current officers compiled information that would be helpful to the next group of officers. They divided the task so that each retiring officer addressed one or two topics. Those notebooks were then given to the new officers. This way, the new officers could quickly see what challenges had been encountered in the past and how past officers were able to address the obstacles. Doing this not only helped the new set of officers get a head start on the year but also kept the advisor from spending extra time each year on topics that had been covered every year in the past.

Saying "Thank You"

One of the biggest problems with Thanksgiving is that the holiday has been reduced to the official starting day of Christmas shopping. We often overlook the importance of stopping to give sincere thanks to others. Saying "thanks" is critically important.

I was a national officer for a large organization of high school and college students. At the national convention at which I was elected, there was a sponsors' night when the organization's numerous sponsors where thanked for their support during the year. Sponsors' names were read, and the audience would give a quick cheer after each. The list was arranged so that the largest contributors were mentioned at the end in order to build excitement.

Three very large automakers were mentioned at the end of that list. When the name "Ford" was read, half the crowd cheered and half booed. When "Chevy" was named, the other half of the crowd cheered and the opposite half booed. This had occurred in the past. It was a friendly rivalry, with both automakers having their loyal fans. In reality, no one should have booed, but I think the sponsors liked the rivalry that had developed.

There was one more automaker that provided sponsorship, though. It happened to be a foreign automaker, and when its name was read, the entire crowd seemed to boo. In essence, the fans loyal to the previous two automakers all booed this third business.

The crowd got caught up in the moment. I'm sure everyone did appreciate the sponsorship from all the businesses, but in that moment, the crowd did something that said "no thanks" instead of "thank you."

Guess who got to go visit that sponsor and try to make amends? Me. I was saved by one very important event. The organization asked its members to send thank-you notes to the automaker to express their sincere thanks for its sponsorship. The company was swamped with thank-you notes.

In fact, the company received so many that someone called to say, "We want you to know that we realize how much our sponsorship means to your members. If you don't mind, could you tell your membership they don't have to send us any more notes? We have to shuffle our schedules in order to free up people to simply open all of the mail!"

Thank-you notes saved the day. It was a powerful way to show sincere appreciation. Don't write thank-you notes just because you want people to keep giving of their time, money, and support. Certainly groups do need assistance from others and thank-you notes help keep this support coming to the group.

Think about what your group would be like if no one took time to volunteer to help you. What experiences would you not have had? What opportunities would not have been available? Write thank-you notes because of the difference others make in your life. Then go out and volunteer so that others can have the same opportunities you so highly value.

I've included a sample thank-you note. This one is a formal, typed thank-you letter.. A hand written thank you would follow the same format but would be shorter in length. The beginning of your thank-you should answer the questions "Who," "What," "When," and "Where." Who are you thanking? Sounds simple, but I've received thank-you notes with my name spelled incorrectly. Nothing says you care like sending a thank-you with the recipient's name misspelled!

If the sponsor was not present at the event, you will need to fully answer the "What," "When," and "Where" questions. The company may sponsor several events, so simply writing "Thank you for sponsoring our leadership day" will not give a clear idea of what the event was or when it took place.

The middle portion of your thank-you answers the question "Why was the support important to the event or group?" The letter should conclude by answering "How will this support affect you and/or the group in the future?"

Answering the "Why" and "How" questions is very important. First, your answers show your sincere appreciation for the support that was provided. Second, by showing your thanks, hopefully the person being thanked will want to help again in the future.

What about simply sending a thank-you note via e-mail? It's certainly not wrong to express your thanks in this way; however, a handwritten thank-you note means much more. I've kept thank-you notes in my journal because the words the person shared were heartfelt and important to me. Sharing the same level of thanks via an e-mail is difficult.

If you take the time to send a thank-you note or letter, do it well. I've received thank-you notes with misspellings or sentences that did not make sense. I knew that the person was in such a hurry to send a card that he or she never even reread the four sentences.

Crossing out or inserting a word in a handwritten note doesn't bother me, but don't just mail a note with errors. This is the equivalent of saying, "I know I need to thank you for this, but it isn't that important, so I'm going to slop through these sentences as fast as possible, mail the note, and cross the task off my list."

Read the note again after you have written it to make sure you haven't left out a word. Make sure the handwriting is legible. You may have sincere words of thanks to share, but if the recipient cannot read them, it doesn't make a difference. If needed, slow down or print the words.

Again, thank-you notes should not be viewed as something you have to do. They should be viewed as something you get to do because you are sincerely thankful for the help that has been given to you. Whenever time is short and you wonder why you are spending so much time on such letters, stop and think what your life or the

October 1, 2007

Mr. Troy Smith
International Enterprises
2155 Berlin Rd.
Suite 5688
Kansas City, MO 64405

Dear Mr. Smith:

**WHAT
WHEN
WHERE**

Thank you for sponsoring our northwest district Emerging
Leaders officer training September 21–22 in Jefferson City.
Over 50 students from all 22 of our chapters attended this
year's event.

The leadership training conference is a very important part
of our officer's year. We are able to learn communication
skills and recruitment techniques that we can use in our
chapters. We participate in teambuilding activities, which we
can take back to our chapters and share with the rest of
our members. We also are given updates about the organization's activities this year.

WHY

This event helps us better lead the members in our local
chapters. These students are able to motivate others to get
involved in contests and participate in leadership events.
The leadership skills also help our members excel in their
many classroom and campus activities.

HOW

Thank you for making this event possible. I truly appreciate
your support and know that I will be a better leader in my
chapter this year because of this training.

Sincerely,

Drew Linell

Drew Linell

organization you represent would be like if not for the help of those you thank. It's usually good inspiration to keep us writing.

I was once asked to volunteer a few hours on a Saturday morning to present a public speaking workshop to 20 eight- to 10-year-old 4-H students. As I was driving to the location, I had doubts about exactly how much I could help third- or fourth-grade students with their speaking skills. I began to doubt why I had even volunteered in the first place. It wasn't that I didn't want to help, but I wondered whether I could help.

The students seemed to really get into the presentation. I kept things simple and fun, and they had a lot of great questions about public speaking that adults don't think to ask. All of the students and many of the parents thanked me for coming when I had concluded.

During the next week, I received a handwritten thank-you note from each one of those students. Their parents may have helped them with the content, but they all had written the notes on their own. I would go back and help the group every year if asked. Why? Because the students made me feel that I really helped, and they showed sincere appreciation for the time I shared with them.

All of us are human. Hopefully we do give of our time and resources to help others. However, I think we all are extra motivated to help when someone shows gratitude. The next time someone helps you, do more than just say "thanks." Write a note, send a card, and sincerely show this person how he or she made a difference. This chapter is all about simple words and steps we can put into practice in order to better lead and serve. It begins by showing thanks.

CHAPTER 6
Teams That Work
ST. JOSEPH, MISSOURI

*"Coming together is the beginning. Keeping together is progress.
Working together is success."*

—HENRY FORD

Each rider was presented with a Bible and recited an oath of allegiance. "While I am in the employ of A. Majors, I agree not use profane language, not to get drunk, not to gamble, not to treat animals cruelly and not to do anything else that is incompatible with the conduct of a gentleman. And I agree, if I violate any of the above conditions, to accept my discharge without any pay for my services."

When the first rider crossed the Missouri River at St. Joseph, Missouri, what lay before him was a relay race of 1,966 miles. It was a race that would last a year and a half and deliver the nation's most important messages from one coast to the other. It was the beginning of the Pony Express.

Russell, Majors, and Waddell founded the Pony Express in 1860 and although the enterprise would not make money, its attempt to deliver news at blazing speeds is still remembered today. The original stables still stand in St. Joseph, casting a shadow on Ninth Street where, ironically, UPS and FedEx trucks speed by, advertising next day delivery before 10:00 a.m.

In 1860, you used the Pony Express when your message absolutely positively had to be there in ten days or less. You paid dearly for such a speedy delivery system. Initially the price was five dollars per one-half ounce, but was later reduced to one dollar per one-half ounce.

The Pony Express "relay" system was remarkable. The nearly two thousand-mile course over the plains and mountains between St. Joseph and Sacramento was dotted with between 150 to 190 stations (only one of those stations is believed to remain on its original site . . . that station is near Hanover, Kansas). Riders received a new horse every ten to fifteen miles. A new rider would take the reins every seventy-five to one hundred miles. Most riders were in their late teens and twenties and were paid one hundred dollars per month.

Those were just the averages. During the history of the Pony Express, several amazing records were set. Bob Haslam once rode an incredible 370-mile shift without a break. The youngest rider was Charlie Miller, who was a mere eleven years old. The fastest trip was seven days seventeen hours from Ft. Kearney, Nebraska, to Placerville, California (the two ends of the telegraph line at the time). The riders were carrying a copy of Lincoln's Inaugural Address.

But as 1860 turned into 1861, the telegraph poles from the east and west grew ever closer, narrowing the gap that a message had to gallop. Eventually those ends of the telegraph line would meet on October 24, 1861. The event meant the end of the Pony Express. It was the conclusion of a great adventure that required the teamwork of hundreds of employees who held a variety of positions need to keep the network running.

Although our means of communication have changed, the workings of the Pony Express still have value as a model of teamwork today. Your team may not be scattered across hundreds of miles, but the team members may be scattered across a campus, city, or state. Certainly they have access to quicker forms of communication, but do they use that communication in a timely fashion? Each employee of the Pony Express had a specific role to play in order for the mail to reach its destination. Each member of your team has specific roles to fulfill if the entire group will reach its goal.

So what do we learn from the Pony Express that we can use today?

Setting the Bar for Excellence

At the beginning of this chapter, I noted that every rider employed by the Pony Express had to recite the following oath: "While I am in the employ of A. Majors, I agree not to use profane language, not to get drunk, not to gamble, not to treat animals cruelly, and not to do anything else that is incompatible with the conduct of a gentleman. And I agree, if I violate any of the above conditions, to accept my discharge without any pay for my services."

It may not sound like much, but it is one of the most important parts of the Pony Express story. The business set a standard for its employees. It was a reasonable set of expectations with a clear consequence if broken. Depending on the type of team you are leading, the complexity of rules will vary, but if you don't have any standards, don't expect people to rise above mediocrity.

I have worked with some teams that had a clear set of guidelines, and all members had to sign their names to show they accepted the rules and the consequences. This is sometimes called a code of conduct. This list will depend on the type of group, but a code of conduct can be important in setting the bar for expected conduct.

This code might contain items such as the percentage of meetings that a person must attend in order to maintain membership. I have been a part of several organizations where I was expected to attend at least 75% of meetings. Such guidelines are not in place to pressure members to do their job but are there to ensure that everyone has an equal stake in the success of the group.

Let's review the rules for scooping manure that I introduced in the second chapter. We've already stressed the importance of rule number one, but for review, here is the entire list.

RULES FOR SCOOPING MANURE

1. The *purpose* for scooping must be well established.
2. *Everyone* should have to take a turn scooping.
3. *Enthusiasm* is critical in creating the best working environment.
4. Developing a *system* makes for efficient and effective work.
5. Sincere *compliments* lay the foundation for future successes.

Even if you have established the purpose in rule number one, violating rule number two will bring the process to a screeching halt. Rule number two is **everyone should have to take a turn scooping**. In other words, the group needs to feel that everyone takes an active role in accomplishing the goal. That's why groups have things like a code of conduct. But it goes beyond what we *have* to do. It is really a matter of what we *should* do if we want to help the team succeed. For those of us in leadership roles, we need to be willing to perform the most menial of jobs when necessary. Consider the following example.

I knew a CEO of a midsized organization who truly believed in not placing himself above the rest of the workforce. Like many businesses of this size, their office had large floors with cubicles for the general workforce. The building had been constructed with "walled" offices with windows along the outside of each floor. These offices were for upper management and meeting space. However, this CEO refused to take one of those offices with a window. He instead sat in a cubicle just like every other ordinary employee. If he had sensitive business that he needed to attend to, he might use a private office for a moment, but then he was right back in his cubicle.

If you want your team to accomplish a difficult task, you have to be willing to do the same work that you ask of everyone else. Your example speaks volumes. Your ability to fulfill this second rule on the list not only helps the task to be accomplished but also serves to inspire others.

My grandfather worked on our farm well into his 90s. I still remember days when he would actively help us drive steel posts for a new fence. He didn't have to do that, but because he did the job, it inspired me to keep working too.

Let's go back to the original manure scooping example. My father is in charge of our farming and ranching operation. Spending all of his time scooping manure in the barns would be silly. He has leadership and management responsibilities that others cannot fulfill.

However, he does invest some time in scooping manure. It not only helps accomplish the task but also allows him to establish better working relationships with all employees. It also helps him keep the perspective of those who do the job. Remember that *perspective* was one of the important qualities necessary in creating the right environment in the green zone.

Finding the Enthusiasm

On our daily radio program, we once featured the organist for a major-league baseball team. Ironically, this lady had not grown up watching the game of baseball. When she was hired to play at the games, she was hired because of her musical abilities, not because she had a good understanding of the game.

This proved to be a bit of a challenge because she didn't always know the right type of music to play at certain points in the game. It wasn't like she was playing "Charge!" when her team struck out, but finding just the right song to capture the spirit of the moment was difficult.

She quickly solved the problem. The room where she played had a window that opened toward the seats on the second deck of the stadium. If she opened the window, she could talk with the fans in the stands. She did just that and began asking them for ideas of songs to play at certain points in the game. She could play anything they might imagine; she just needed to know what songs would be best.

Her role is to build enthusiasm for the team. That is really the entire reason an organist plays at a game. As human beings, we place a lot of importance on the cheers of the crowd. After all, why is there such a thing as home field advantage? Why do odds-makers give teams an advantage when they play on their own court? Nothing about the field, the court, or the players changes; only the surroundings change. The enthusiasm of the crowd is counted as an advantage to the home team.

Being enthusiastic when things are going well is easy, but great leaders master the art of keeping a good attitude when things go poorly. This does *not* mean that you overlook obvious problems just to keep a good attitude. It *does* mean that you deal with obstacles while seeking to maintain a positive environment.

I was once conducting a radio interview in Montana with a Lewis and Clark historian. One of this gentleman's particular interests was music, so we discussed the expedition and the singing and dancing the men engaged in on their two-and-a-half-year trip in 1804–1806. At one point I asked, "So when did they sing? Did they have a set time in the evening when someone would begin singing?"

Frustrated, the historian said to me, "No, no, you just don't understand. This is not like today, when guys say, 'Sing? No, my wife sings but not me. I'm no good.' Singing was a guy thing. They sang all the time, in happy times and in sad times. It was part of their life."

Singing was something the men on the expedition did to build enthusiasm. The work was long and hard. It was so difficult that boils

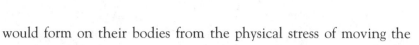

would form on their bodies from the physical stress of moving the expedition up the Missouri River and over the Rocky Mountains. Singing was a form of enthusiasm that kept the team moving forward.

Enthusiasm for work and life is vital. My mother has taught fourth grade for many years. One of the subjects she teaches is improper fractions. If you've forgotten what an improper fraction is, it is a number such as 5/4. It is when the larger number is over a smaller number, hence the name "improper."

This can be a difficult concept for some fourth graders to understand. When learning fractions, we often use the example of slices of a pie. The number 1/6 could be represented by one out of six slices of a pie. But with a number like 5/4, the pie example doesn't work very well. The students can't understand how you can shove five pieces of pie in a plate that will hold only four.

One day my mom was really struggling with the topic. One little boy, Matt, just couldn't understand improper fractions. Next to Matt was an empty student's desk, so my mom stepped up on the chair and then stood on the desk. Imagine a fourth-grade teacher standing on student's desk in the middle of her classroom.

"Should I be standing on this desk, Matt?" she asked.

Matt and the other students didn't say anything but just shook their heads back and forth to say "no," yet they were still puzzled by their teacher standing on top of the desk at the front of the classroom.

"Of course, I shouldn't be on top of the desk. I'm bigger than the desk. This is improper because the bigger thing is standing on top of the smaller thing. It's just like improper fractions. The bigger number is over the smaller number. You've got more pie than the plate can hold."

Immediately the class understood the concept of improper fractions. My mom still stands on top of a desk every year when she teaches improper fractions. Her enthusiasm for the topic helps students better

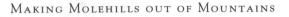

understand the concept. Sometimes each of us needs to stand on a desk and add a little enthusiasm to what we do.

What can you do to add life to life itself? You don't have to have a gimmick or be insincere. Simply look for the best in each situation. I'm definitely not telling you to ignore things that are wrong or not to do what's difficult. Great leaders are able to sustain enthusiasm even in times when things don't go the way they should.

Proverbs 17:22 says, "A merry heart doeth good like a medicine." The enthusiasm you share is truly like a medicine. The preceding examples show the difference that a spark can make in everyday life.

We'll discuss enthusiasm under pressure more in the "Complaints and Compliments" section that follows.

Developing the System

The Pony Express is a great model of building a system that gets work done efficiently and effectively. The network of stations provided the needed riders and horses with a way to move the mail across the nation. Rule number four is **develop a system that makes for efficient and effective work**.

We found that cleaning manure can be a difficult job. The chute that is used for vaccinating cattle has sensors underneath it that can read an animal's weight. If manure builds up under the chute, the sensors my quit working. This is a very difficult place to clean, so we made our own specialized tools that can slide under the chute and quickly clean around the sensors.

In fact, we have several tools that we use in order to scoop manure. We found that you can't just use an ordinary scoop to *scoop* manure! In order to accomplish your mission, your team will need several different tools. The team needs to feel it has the freedom to suggest and implement ideas. If you have done a good job of implementing rules one, two, and three, the team will be much more willing to suggest, adopt, and implement new ideas.

That doesn't necessarily mean that there are shortcuts to get you to where you need to be, but it does mean that you need to implement detailed processes that can move you toward a goal. In this case, what needs to be accomplished truly amounts to a mountain. Yet we implement a system and we effectively utilize the skills of others to reduce the lofty goal to the size of a molehill.

I was working on an assignment at the Martin Guitar Company that taught me a lot about how individual steps can form an overall process that produces great results.

While the world around it has changed since it was founded in 1833, much of the skilled craftsmanship needed to make guitars remains just as it did when C. F. Martin founded his business. One of the best parts about the factory is the fact that it is open to the public. Before I sat down to interview George Molchany, one of the long-time craftsmen at Martin, he suggested that we take a quick look at the guitar-making process.

Martin takes great pride in fashioning the best in the business. George went on to back up his statement by telling me that producing great-sounding guitars is definitely not a quick process.

As he explained, there are over three hundred specific operations that have to be performed. Some of these operations are quite detailed and take much time. At one point in the process, you will still see hundreds of clothespins used to hold strips of lining onto the body of the guitars. Some intricate pearl inlay work may require a craftsman to spend well over ten hours of work on just one instrument.

This is the type of work where a sixteenth of an inch seems like a mile. Wood chisels and sandpaper are still very important tools of the trade. "Hand" work is the only type of work that will do in most cases.

Probably the most important part of the entire process comes when the neck, or handle, of the guitar is fitted onto the body. The fit must be perfect in order for the guitar to play and sound its best. This requires fine rasps, files, and sandpaper.

Finally, the guitar reaches George. He is step number three hundred. This is a great position, because it is here that George becomes the first person to play the instrument. He smiled and said, "The guitar becomes a playable instrument in my hands and that is a good feeling. The pride alone when you see the finished product is very rewarding."

Leadership is not a quick and easy process. Greatness is shaped and molded over years. Experience takes off the rough edges and helps us "get in tune" with others. After three hundred steps, a new Martin guitar has a unique sound regarded as tops in the industry. Time, experience, and patience are qualities sometimes overlooked in a fast-paced world, yet they are the very qualities that bring forth greatness. These qualities help shape unique people—and items—that have special qualities you just can't find anywhere else. As George says, "You just can't rush a good thing."

Complaints and Compliments

Despite our best attempts to facilitate good teamwork, sometimes things might not go right. We won't always be able to put differing sides back together quickly, but each of us can do things to work together, even when our ideas may seem to be worlds apart.

I once did a series of interviews at Atlanta's Hartsfield-Jackson International Airport. Richard is a complaint resolution agent, and his job is literally to handle complaints all day long. It's about more than simply finding solutions, though; it's about building relationships that create loyal customers.

That's an important point to keep in mind when bringing sides together. Does the solution simply solve the problem in the present, or does it seek to create a meaningful difference in the future as well?

One day, a flight was oversold, and it was up to Richard to reticket several passengers. Spirits were low, and some people had directed their anger toward Richard. He decided to turn the gatehouse into a game show. Instead of *The Price Is Right*, Richard called the show *The Flight Is Right*. When it was time for a passenger to get his or her new ticket, he would call out the individual's name and shout, "Come on down! You're the next contestant on *The Flight Is Right!*"

One young mother's name was called, and her toddler in a diaper followed along behind her. The two were quite excited, and the mother picked up the child and placed her on the ticket counter. As the passengers gave a round of applause, the child's diaper fell off. Richard says it was the most memorable moment he has had in his 23 years as an agent.

"We try to empathize and put ourselves in the customer's shoes. I handle the customer just like I would want to be treated," he said. Richard also hopes people realize that "in life, we always have things that are going to go wrong no matter what we do." You can't expect good fortune every minute of every day. When tough problems arise, stay calm, be patient, and begin looking for solutions.

On the basis of interviews with people like Richard and many others in the field of customer service, I've found the following three steps to mending fences:

1. "I have a voice." People want to know that they can share their ideas, complaints, suggestions, and thoughts. Nothing is more frustrating than having something important on your mind and yet no one seems to care about you or what you have to say.

2. "I am heard." It doesn't matter whether you have a voice if you aren't heard. Being heard requires more than just passive listening. We must ask questions of the other person to better understand his or her point of view. We can't address the situation if we fail to understand the problem in the first place.

3. "I am a part of the solution." If I'm able to share my thoughts and if I'm truly heard, then the solution should address at least some of my original complaint. If I'm not complaining but instead offering ideas, the group's idea should include my input.

If someone has a voice and is heard yet you can't give him or her an adequate solution, then you better have a reasonable reason why. I have a friend who is a Secret Service agent. He once told me that when he is on security detail, people sometimes get frustrated because they are not allowed to enter certain restricted areas. He quickly learned that instead of just telling someone, "You can't come in here," it works much better to give people a simple explanation why and to tell them when they will be allowed to enter or give them a good alternative.

You don't have to be a Secret Service agent to put this into practice. Our family was eating at a local pizza place. We ordered a family deal that included pizza, drinks, and breadsticks. I noticed that a soda cost more than a side salad. I didn't care to have a soda, so I asked whether I could substitute a salad instead, especially because it was less expensive.

I was told, "The manager said no substitutions are allowed." Notice that steps one and two above had been accomplished. I did have a voice, and I was heard. My idea was reasonable. It would not cost the pizza place more money but less. My idea was not a part of the solution, and no adequate reason was given to me.

A minute later the server came back to me and said, "I don't see why we can't substitute a salad for a soda, especially because it costs less money." She had thought about the problem and realized the answer she had given really didn't make sense. Her answer more than satisfied me because I now felt that my idea not only had been heard but also was part of the solution. She also received a bigger tip from our family because of her service!

Sustaining enthusiasm can be difficult when you feel pressure or are handling complaints. However, if you keep in mind the three points above, you will better be able to handle difficult situations and find win-win solutions.

Strengths and Weaknesses

The object of having a good team, of course, is combining individual strengths to create a better whole. Knowing the individuals on your team and their natural talents is important. If you aren't in a leadership role, you can still be willing to offer your skills when an opportunity arises. In large groups, it may be difficult for leadership to know everyone's skills, though.

Consider the leaders of the great expedition to the Pacific Ocean. In 1803 as Lewis and Clark were preparing for their journey to the Pacific Ocean and back, the leaders of the Corps of Discovery readied their men at a camp just north of St. Louis. Meriwether Lewis had been appointed by President Jefferson to lead the mission, but Lewis secured the help of an old acquaintance, William Clark.

Although Lewis had a higher rank than Clark, he fabricated his rank and made him a captain as well. The men in the expedition were told that both commanders carried equal authority. Lewis realized his shortcomings when choosing Clark. Lewis has been described as introverted and even a bit of a nerd, the type of person who would put on two different-colored socks and not notice. He spent time in St. Louis and secured the supplies needed for the expedition.

Clark, on the other hand, was an expert at working with others. People skills were one of his talents. He knew how to levy discipline when needed and how to bring a team together. During the winter of 1803–1804, Clark was drilling his men at their winter camp. Two men got into a fight, and Clark had to hand down the discipline.

Instead of giving a sentence of lashes, the usual punishment, he had an unusual assignment for the two. He ordered the two men to work together to build a house for the woman who lived there and did their washing. The two had to get along if they wanted to complete the task. It was imperative they get along. On their journey they would be around each other every single day.

Team building sometimes requires us to do what is difficult. The object is to provide strong leadership but also to work to get along and direct the team to complete the mission. Lewis and Clark combined their strengths to make it happen. We should do likewise.

It's Often the Little Things

One important part of this book is demonstrating how little changes can have large and lasting impacts. The final rule for scooping manure is **sincere *compliments* lay the foundation for future successes**. In producing my daily radio broadcasts for more than a decade, I've literally seen the difference those little things can have on a workplace, an organization, or a family.

I had the opportunity to interview Fred Mares, greeter "extraordinaire" at the Hy-Vee supermarket in Maryville, Missouri. Although he has many other duties beyond just saying "hello" to those who enter the store, his ability to build relationships with customers is what has won the store loyal patrons and made Fred well known to those in his community.

Fred truly defines what it is to do a job well. He goes far beyond a simple smile when someone enters. He begins by introducing himself, and he eventually learns the names of the many people who shop there. Soon he is calling people by their first names and taking a sincere interest in their lives. It isn't uncommon for Fred to ask about someone's relative who is ill or about a new grandchild in the family. When people see Fred, he is like another member of the family.

Fred shares that one of his secrets is reading all of the local newspapers. He looks at birth notices, community awards, events, and even obituaries. He often sends a card of congratulations to his customers when something good happens to them or their family. He has been known to personally travel to a funeral visitation at night just to pay his respects to a customer who has lost a loved one.

One day Fred noticed how many foreign-exchange students from the local university came to Hy-Vee to buy their groceries. These young people spoke English as a second language, and they were often too shy to ask questions. Fred took it upon himself to learn simple phrases in all of their native languages. They are often surprised to find Fred speaking familiar words to them when they enter the store!

Fred builds relationships by focusing on the needs of others and making them feel at home and truly caring about more than just what groceries they purchase. People are often fascinated to learn that he is an accomplished writer and even won a Pulitzer Prize for reporting at the *Kansas City Star*.

Fred says the key to building these relationships is really found in the little things. He is sure to say "please" and "thank you" to other employees every time they assist him with something around the store. He knows that building lasting relationships is about far more than just saying "hello." It requires the extra effort to truly get to know others and help meet their needs. Little things make a huge difference!

CHAPTER 7
What Really Matters
STILLWATER, OKLAHOMA

*"It is right to be contented with what we have,
never with what we are."*

—SIR JAMES MACKINTOSH

The clock that hung high above the court at Okalahoma State University's Gallagher-Iba Arena still showed more than 30 minutes before game time when I sat down at the end of the bench to visit with the coaches. My broadcast work had taken me to this venue to capture the story of one individual's rise to success in the game of basketball.

Coach Jill Nagel was never a highly recruited athlete. In fact, she was never recruited as an athlete. She related to me what life was like for her, growing up while attending a small rural high school where everyone who went out for the basketball team made the squad. Although it was a small school, it had a tradition of fielding good boys' and girls' teams, some of which had advanced far into the state play-offs.

But Nagel was far from a star. In her first year, she spent the majority of her time at the end of the bench. Her time on the court came only in the final minutes of lopsided wins or losses. Between her sophomore and junior years, she set the goal to start on the varsity team. Everybody laughed at such a goal. She wasn't a very good athlete, and the team certainly had plenty of girls who were better than she was.

She spent the summer and fall running extra sprints and shooting hundreds of baskets. She voluntarily ran drills over and over again in an effort to make her dream come true. When her junior year arrived, the hard work did pay off. She started every game that year on a team that won their conference's championship.

That team was largely composed of seniors, and with their graduation, prospects for the team were not good. In fact, Nagel was the only returning starter. Once again she set new goals, both individually and for the team. She vowed that the team would go further in the play-offs than it had the year before. Again, everyone laughed knowing that all of the talent had graduated.

Nagel spent another year voluntarily running sprints and drills and shooting more jumpers than she had shot in the rest of her life combined. That team amazed the locals, going further in the play-offs than the previous year. Nagel was a first team all-conference selection and led the team in scoring.

Those were nice accolades, but if she had any hopes of continuing her basketball career, she faced one major obstacle. Not one single college recruiter had ever come to watch her play, and she hadn't received any scholarship offers to play for even the smallest of colleges. Now people really laughed at her goal of playing basketball at the collegiate level. "She won't play in one single game," they said to themselves.

After four years of college, those who had those thoughts were absolutely correct. She had not played in one single game. In fact, after four years at William Jewell College, she had played in *every* game but one. She had played in 128 of 129 games and during that time had set her college's record for three-point percentage and had been selected as an all-conference honorable mention athlete.

From there, she went on to try out for three WNBA teams, the highest level of women's professional basketball in the country. Her dedication to the sport had also led her to coach at the Division I level of women's collegiate basketball, and on this night, as assistant coach and lead recruiter, her team was on the road to play the Cowgirls of Oklahoma State.

It was certainly inspiring to sit on the bench and recall the story of how Nagel had gone from that small high school and no college scholarships to now coach on the sidelines of an important game in one of the nation's largest arenas. But, you see, the story holds even more significance to me because I knew Coach Nagel when she was in high school. Her maiden name is Jill McCrea, and she is my sister.

One important lesson each of us needs to learn about life and leadership is that success is often found in the little things. Great leaders do the little things that turn into big things. They have the perseverance and belief in their overall purpose to keep doing the little things until big things happen. That is what my sister's route to the WNBA demonstrated. Running sprints and shooting baskets one afternoon really didn't make a big difference. Running sprints and shooting baskets every afternoon for 10 years made a BIG difference.

In this chapter we focus on the red zone of leadership development. This is the area of maximum efficiency and effectiveness. Achievements in this zone come as a result of successes in the green and yellow zones.

The goal is not to live in the red zone, though. Climbers cannot live on the summit of Mount Everest. The conditions are too harsh. The amount of oxygen in the air is about a third less than normal. Likewise, if we attempt to live our entire lives in the red zone, we will most likely produce unhealthy stress in our lives.

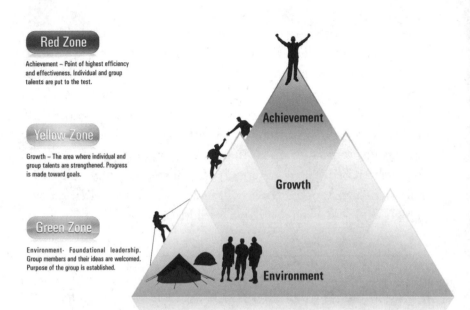

Red Zone

Achievement – Point of highest efficiency and effectiveness. Individual and group talents are put to the test.

Yellow Zone

Growth – The area where individual and group talents are strengthened. Progress is made toward goals.

Green Zone

Environment· Foundational leadership. Group members and their ideas are welcomed. Purpose of the group is established.

Achievement

Growth

Environment

Some stress is good. The adage in weightlifting is true: "No pain, no gain." For example, if my maximum bench press is 250 pounds, I might lift between 175 and 225 pounds for a good workout. My maximum press of 250 pounds represents my red zone. I can't workout at that weight. However, constant work in the yellow zone, my "growth zone" of 175 to 225 pounds, will ultimately help me push my maximum bench press even higher. The same concept is true for other parts of our life.

Climber Alan Hobson told me something very important about his climb to Everest's summit. He compared it to our biggest achievements in life. "The average climber stands there for 15 minutes," he said. Yet it takes three to seven years to prepare for that journey. "I'll save you the mental math," he continued. "Three to seven years for 15 minutes equals one-quarter-millionth of the time. One-quarter-millionth of the time we spend preparing for our big dreams in life do we actually get to experience them."

Perhaps I study for four or five years to get my college degree, yet walking across the stage to accept my diploma takes only a moment. Or maybe we invest 18 years in raising a child to someday see that moment when he or she walks across the stage to get a high school diploma.

There are approximately 450 mountain peaks over 23,000 feet in height. The skills you learn climbing any one of those peaks will largely transfer to climbing any other one. Certainly each peak is different, yet the skills required are much the same. The same is true in life. When we make it our goal to expand our abilities by living in the yellow zone, we gain the experience we need to hit the summit in the red zone.

Hitting the red zone does take time and effort; any worthwhile goal does. If you want to climb a peak that is more than 23,000 feet high, you will have to travel to Asia. The highest peak on any other continent is Aconcagua in Argentina, which is just over 22,800 feet. The tallest peak in North America is Mount McKinley (Denali) at more than 20,300 feet. Our greatest goals in life require us to move outside of our comfort zones and take on new challenges. Whether the goal requires us to travel a physical distance or just cover a large gap in our current abilities, we should set our sites on a summit and then develop the skills that will help us push into the red zone some day to conquer that peak.

We should never believe that we are too young or too old to begin the process. In 2003 a 70-year-old man and a 15-year-old girl both reached the summit of Everest, making them the oldest and youngest climbers, respectively, to achieve the feat. One Sherpa has made 16 treks to the summit, the most of any climber. Young or old, experienced or novice, we can begin to take steps now that will help us reach our biggest goals.

Little Things Add Up

What we often fail to realize is that "small" decisions we make every day create major differences in our lives and dramatically affect what we achieve. Consider the following example.

Every day two people are given $3 apiece. This money is an extra bonus tacked onto their normal salaries. They can do whatever they like with this extra money. They will continue to receive the extra $3 every day for the rest of their lives.

Person A takes that extra money and saves it. At the end of one year, he has $1,095. He decides to invest this savings to see whether he can earn an extra return. He invests it into a mutual fund that has a long track record of success. For our example, this mutual fund has an annual return of 10%. There are several mutual funds with well over a 10 year track record of 12% annual returns or more. Person A continues to take the $3 he gets every day and puts it into this fund.

At the end of 10 years he now has more than $19,000. After 30 years he has almost $200,000. After 50 years of repeating this same process every day, he now has more than $1.4 million! The following table demonstrates how savings do add up over time.

Time	Account Balance
	$3/day @ 10% interest
1 Year	$1,095
10 Years	$19,196
20 Years	$68,987
30 Years	$198,133
40 Years	$533,103
50 Years	$1,401,928

Leaving a leadership legacy is not a matter of chance. The outcome is largely within your control. Those outcomes are mostly based on the habits we develop. In the previous example two people were "given" $3 each day. Let's make a small change to the example. Instead of earning an extra $3 per day, each person now finds an area of his or her life where he or she will no longer spend $3 or more each day. Stop and think about your average day or week. What small thing(s) could you cut out of your life in order to save $3?

Studies show that 88% of those Americans who have saved $1 million or more are first-generation millionaires. In other words, most didn't achieve this status because they were given a head start in life. They got there because they began to apply beneficial habits over time.

If you don't think habits can affect a person's life, look at the following chart. This graph shows the leading causes of death in the United States. By far, the two leading causes of death are tobacco and poor diet/inactivity. If I go out and smoke a pack of cigarettes today, it is highly unlikely I will die tonight from that. If I go eat 10 pieces of strawberry cheesecake and spend the rest of the day on the couch while watching television, it is unlikely I will die tonight from overeating and not exercising. However, if I make these activities

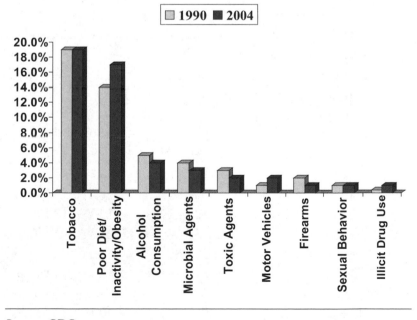

Source: CDC

habits, they will very likely lead to major health problems and reduce my life expectancy.

The great irony of life is that the things that usually do us in are not things that happen suddenly; they are things that we do to ourselves over time. **The time to put habits into practice is now!** Sure, you can wait 10 years to save money. You don't have to watch your weight and exercise right now. Maybe you say that you will quit smoking some day. But people usually have a very hard time breaking these actions because they become habits, and those habits are already influencing the future.

I hope you will decide not to smoke. I hope that you will eat smart and make time to stay active.I hope you don't feel you have to drink alcohol to fit in or be accepted. It's my desire that you will even be a bit of a nerd and make it your goal to save at least $3 a day. If you do this, you will not only develop the habits that will make you more financially secure but likely add years to your life.

Just as I demonstrated that saving money has a compound effect that can help you become a millionaire, the opposite habit can lead you to a lifetime of financial despair. Consider what happens if you decide to have a credit card and don't pay the balance each month.

Balance Owed	Interest Rate	Minimum Payment %	Total Interest Paid	Time to Pay Balance
$1,000	10.00%	2	$1,506	10 Yrs. 4 Months
$1,000	15.00%	2	$2,123	14 Yrs. 3 Months
$1,000	18.00%	2	$2,931	19 Yrs. 3 Months
$5,000	10.00%	2	$3,364	21 Yrs. 10 Months
$5,000	15.00%	2	$7,789	32 Yrs 1 Months
$5,000	18.00%	2	$13,931	46 Yrs. 1 Months
$10,000	10.00%	2	$6,935	26 Yrs. 8 Months
$10,000	15.00%	2	$16,123	39 Yrs. 8 Months
$10,000	18.00%	2	$28,931	57 Yrs. 7 Months

Just for fun, let's say you are an 18-year-old high school senior reading this book. Prom is just around the corner and you are making plans for the event. You want to hit the town in style. First you find the perfect dress or get the perfect tuxedo. Then you decide to rent a limo for the evening. Now figure in the cost of the meal, the flowers, and all the extras to impress your date.

You're short on cash, but that's not a problem because you will put it on your credit card and pay it off later. The total bill comes to about $1,000 (to some of you this total seems ridiculously high; to others it is ridiculously small. It is pretty easy to spend $1,000 on the prom and/or graduation, so let's go with it). You are just a senior in high school, so you didn't get the greatest interest rate for the card. The rate is 22%.

Prom is over, and you graduate and head on to college or into the working world. Money is tight, so you just keep paying the minimum payment of 2% on that credit card. Somehow you never seem to be able to pay more than that minimum payment. No big deal, though; it's costing you an average of only $15 a month to satisfy the company.

The day finally arrives to make the final payment on that card. How long did it take you to pay for the prom? Imagine toting a couple of grandchildren with you to the mailbox as at the age of 64 you send the check to make that last payment on your prom! Yes, paying the minimum payment in this situation would result in you being 64 years of age when making the final payment and in the original $1,000 bill costing you $6,366 in interest. Your senior prom just cost you $7,366 and 46 years of your life to pay it off. You are a senior citizen when you pay for your senior prom!

The situation is not as far fetched as you might think. Poor habits can cause this scenario to be far too close to reality. Just as personal savings can swell over the years, your debts can swallow you as well. That's why developing habits to avoid debt is critical. Will this be easy to do? Not always. Developing good habits takes commitment. Those habits stretch beyond finances and reach into all areas of our lives.

Consider the story of a man named James. His father died when he was only 18 months old, and his passing left his mother, brother, and two sisters to work the farm and garden to make a living. As James grew to school age, his mother saw potential in the young man and knew that he needed an education. The only problem was that they couldn't afford to send him to school. So, between his mother and his brother, they were able to scrape up $17, which sent him to school for one year.

The $17 education was equivalent to earning a high school diploma. At Geauga Seminary he eventually earned the diploma. James was about 16 years old at the time, and he soon began an alternating-semester pattern of work and school, his own system for paying his way through college. At one time, he even worked as the school janitor to make the money to earn his education. James was once quoted as saying, "A pound of pluck is worth a ton of luck," a testament to his hardworking attitude.

So who did James become? President of the United States James Garfield, a man who earned his college education by going to school in alternating semesters so that he could pay for his classes—a man who was willing to be a janitor so he cold become president of the United States. Hard work combined with good habits can help leaders achieve more and leave a legacy of leadership.

The Cost of Our Decisions

Think about it. A habit you develop right now can already have a big impact in just 10 years. In an earlier example, a person saved $3 per day. We labeled that individual "Person A." "Person B" also has the ability to save $3. She, however, is a smoker and uses the $3 to purchase a pack of cigarettes every day. She makes a decent living, but she isn't saving the extra money like person A. **At the end of 10 years, the cost of her decision has been more than $18,000.**

Just so we are clear, person B has now waived the opportunity to save money, in essence spending $18,000 on cigarettes. *However,* there is a much bigger cost. The result of her decision has more than doubled her risk of cancer. She is more likely to get sick. Her insurance premiums are higher, and her life expectancy is reduced. The cost of the "small" decision long ago has been very high indeed. This person has just turned a molehill into a mountain, the exact opposite result we are working toward.

At this point, people always have some objections to the above example. "I don't want to wait 50 years to get my $1.4 million," they say. Me neither. So why don't you save $6 each day and get there in less than half the time?

"I don't have someone to give me six extra dollars," they respond. That's right—no one is just going to hand you six extra dollars each day. So how do you get that extra money? Look at your life and find a place where you can save $6 each day. "But I need every single dollar I make," you may say. Certainly some times during our lives won't be easy. However, remember that James Garfield had nothing, yet he was willing to work his way through school just to get the education he desired.

Saving money instead of buying cigarettes has easily identifiable outcomes. What about little things that often go unnoticed, though? What if I spent 30 minutes every other day working out instead of watching television? Perhaps I could spend 15 minutes each morning before work or school reading a book that would help me grow. Or what if I got a book on CD or downloaded a podcast and listened to it in the car? **Identify and invest in habits that will have long-term payoffs. Great leaders do.**

My experience has been that people usually have two reasons for why they do not put into practice the above habits. One, people find it hard to begin making choices that won't immediately produce visible results. This requires discipline. It is a characteristic that great leaders share. My sister ran extra sprints in high school not knowing that it would produce a tryout for the WNBA in 10 years.

Can't you just begin these habits later in life? When it comes to money, you might say, "I'll make more money in the future and just begin saving it then." Let's take a look at that point of view. The following table assumes that you are able to save $10 per day. It also assumes that you receive a 10% annual return on your money.

Time	Account Balance
	$10/day @ 10% interest
1 Year	$3,650
10 Years	$63,989
34.5 Years	$1,035,654
41.5 Years	$2,056,288
45.5 Years	$3,029,245
50 Years	$4,673,093

In this example, a person accumulates $1 million in 34.5 years. *However*, to accumulate the next million takes only seven years, and the third million takes only another four years. The power of compounding interest is clearly seen in the example. It takes time to get the savings ball rolling, but given two or three decades, the savings really begin to multiply.

Time is the key factor here. If a person wanted to save $1 million and do it in just 10 years at the same rate of interest (10%), he or she would need to save just over $158 per day, or $58,000 per year, to achieve the goal! There's a big difference between saving $3,650 per year and saving $58,000 per year. No matter what area of your life needs improvement, begin now. The investments you make in your life now will pay even bigger returns in the future.

Here's the point: if later in life you are able to save more than $58,000 annually, great. But why not begin by saving just $10 a day now? Time is the critical factor. Once you live it, you can't get that time back.

The second reason we often don't begin practicing good habits now is that we lack the strength to continue the habit in the face of those who ridicule us. Leadership is influence. Your actions are viewed by others. What you do or don't do can have a big impact on others. Standing by such decisions requires strength.

Remember that people laughed at my sister for practicing basketball so much. She could have wilted under the ridicule. Why didn't she? She had a clear sense of her purpose and goals for life. That kept her focused on the habits that would bring her success.

Benjamin Franklin said, "Little leaks sink big ships." Investing in leadership requires looking at the "little leaks" in your own life, shoring up the ship, and sailing toward the intended direction.

Common leaks come in many forms. These are little things we don't often think about, such as the extra half hour of television we watch or the physical workout we fail to do. Think of your life as a bank account. How can you invest in making yourself the best person you can be?

Don't rely on good fortune, karma, or lady luck to work magic in your favor. If instead of saving $10 each day you spent that money on Power Ball tickets, at the end of 50 years, you would have purchased $182,620 worth of tickets (this even takes into account leap years). The odds of any one ticket winning the Power Ball grand prize are 1 in 146,107,962. Purchasing 182,620 tickets would improve your odds of winning the grand prize to just over 1 in 8,000.

Too many times we pin our hopes on things like a 1-in-8,000 chance of hitting it big. In reality, we must be dedicated to positive leadership habits that will drive us toward goals we could have only imagined when we began our journey.

It's Not Really about the Money

Up to this point, we've spent a large portion of this chapter using financial savings to demonstrate the importance of investing in yourself and your future. Building wealth is great, but leadership isn't really about money. It's not about becoming famous or having people notice you. **It's not about what you get but what you give.**

There probably never has been a journey that taught me as much about filling our unique roles as a trip I made across the border south of San Diego to Tijuana, Mexico. A team of about fifteen people was headed into the border city to visit an orphanage and assist with medical check-ups for the kids there. I was a little nervous about helping out, not because I didn't want to be of service, but because I didn't know any Spanish and I had never been to this orphanage before. I really wondered if I had any skills to offer.

Soon I felt like the equivalent of the last kid picked when dividing teams on the playground. I just didn't have anything to offer. Everyone else was really good at something, but I excelled at nothing. Five medical doctors were working with our group, and how I wished I were a doctor. I didn't even speak Spanish, so I was no use as a translator. What on earth was I going to do?

"Andrew, I've got a job for you," said the leader of the trip as she finished assisting one of the doctors with setting up his exam area.

"What do you have for me?" I replied, expecting it to be some aspect of helping the doctor.

"I'm going to take you over to the room where all the boys at the orphanage stay. You can keep them entertained before they have to come visit the doctor," she replied.

My heart sank. "Keep them entertained?" I thought to myself. I sure was vital to the trip, wasn't I? If ever there was something that said, "You're unimportant," it was to be asked to keep kids entertained.

We walked across a small courtyard to a plain, unpainted door, behind which I could hear the screams of what seemed to be a playground full of children, except for the fact that all the noise was coming from inside the room instead of outside. What could be behind that door? Exactly how many kids were there?

"The orphanage has about fifteen three- to eight-year-old boys. They'll be glad to see you. There's only one girl to look after all of them." With that the leader opened the door to what instantly became a mad rush of children climbing on top of me. Within two seconds I had children swinging from my arms and attached to my legs. As one fell off an arm, another jumped on, and other kids climbed to the top of their bunk beds for a chance to leap onto my back. I was a morsel of food under attack by a swarm of ants determined to devour me!

One thing I quickly learned is that you don't need to know much Spanish to entertain a group of kids in a Mexican orphanage. I also learned that nothing will wear you out more quickly than trying to keep an entire orphanage entertained before the "scary" trip to the doctor. When I emerged from the room three hours later, I appeared to have done battle with a pack of wolves.

I was later told that the role I played that day might have been the most important of all to those boys. While the medical check-ups were vital in assuring their health and the translators were needed to relay that information to the children and supervisors, the staff at the orphanage was so small that it was rare an adult had time to play games with the boys. In addition, the staff was entirely female, so it had been a long time since a male was there to entertain those boys, a role I filled that day.

We are sometimes tempted to feel that we have nothing to offer, yet we have so much to share in a multitude of ways. Before I met my wife, she spent two full years in Bolivia where she served as a volunteer with a program through her church. She still volunteers there during the summer as a translator on medical missions to the country. On her first trip to the small town where she spends much of her time, she saw a little girl playing in the street. The girl wore a pretty necklace that appeared to be homemade. Paula stopped and complimented the girl on the beautiful necklace she wore. The girl stopped, reached behind her neck, and unclasped the chain, and with an outstretched hand, she offered it to Paula.

I am always amazed that people who have the least seem willing to give the most. Each one of us can give in our own unique way. Some people may not care much about the savings and credit card payment tables in this chapter. Making money and becoming wealthy aren't my top goals, either. However, I do believe that we should be responsible stewards of what God has given us. That includes looking at how we can use our skills to help others.

Make it a goal to volunteer for organizations and contribute to charities. No matter how little you may think you have to give, you will find that you can be just as the little girl in Bolivia who was willing to give up her necklace. It is more blessed to give than to receive. You will find tremendous joy in helping others. Even if you cannot give of your money, give of your time. Each one of us can always share of our time and talents.

Use the tools in this book to get money and then give it away. Use the tips to gain time and then give it to your family, friends, or worthy causes. Develop a plan to create the best "you" that you can.

While you do this, use your abilities to help others! That is what this chapter is all about. It is about living your life so that it continues to affect others.

I have talked briefly in this book about living a balanced life in the social, mental, physical, and spiritual areas of your life. Let me take just a moment to speak to the spiritual component of your life. I realize that there are a lot of things in this world that I cannot understand or control. My faith is what ultimately gives me hope for the future both now and eternally.

I do hope that you will not forget about this very important component of your life. My book *God's Perfect View* speaks to ways we can grow in our spiritual life. Do not think that the brief amount of time we have spent discussing faith means that it is a trivial part of life. Far from it. That's why I wrote an entire book about it.

Conclusion

Perhaps leadership is not so much about the mountains and the molehills as it is about simply beginning to climb. My sister was working toward her goal, but it was ultimately the climb itself that prepared her to accomplish so much in life today. That climb ultimately prepared her for far more than just a tryout for the WNBA. What we find in the pursuit of our dreams is far more than we could have imagined. In essence, our leadership journey comes full circle as we realize that our trip is about both the destination and the drive. It is about both the mountain and the climb.

So what is your dream? What little things are you doing to get there? Set your destination and begin the drive. Fix your sights and begin the climb.